FRIED-EGG SANDWICHES & OTHER COMFORTS OF HOME

Fried-Egg Sandwiches
& Other Comforts of Home

Stories That Nourish the Soul

RICHARD SPEIGHT

DIMENSIONS
FOR LIVING
NASHVILLE

FRIED-EGG SANDWICHES
AND OTHER COMFORTS OF HOME

Copyright © 1996 by Richard Speight

This book is printed on acid-free, recycled paper.

Library of Congress Cataloging-in-Publication Data

Speight, Richard.
    Fried-egg sandwiches and other comforts of home/Richard Speight.
      p.   cm.
    ISBN 0-687-00238-9 (alk. paper)
    1. Christian life—Ancedotes. 2. Speight, Richard. I. Title.
    BV4517.S64   1996
    242—dc20   95-42826

95 96 97 98 99 00 01 02 03 04 – 10 9 8 7 6 5 4 3 2 1

For Barbara,
my wife for thirty-two years,
my sweetheart even longer,
my friend, advisor, and editor from the beginning,
and my soul mate forever.
Without her my books would not be here,
nor would I.
I thank God for her every single day.

CONTENTS

George and the Bandit Box

— . —

THE THREE THINGS I REMEMBER MOST about George are his red hair, his freckled face, and his smile. I also remember how nicely those three things blended together.

I don't know what goes on in heaven when a baby is about to be sent to earth, but I imagine the angels had a rather easy task on their hands when they put George together. As soon as they scattered those freckles all over his face, they no doubt knew that he simply *had* to have red hair. And he certainly was going to need a disarming smile.

George's hair wasn't a bright red, or a flaming red, or anything like that—it was more like the color of an orange tabby cat. Indeed, when a feisty tabby moved in with us and adopted one of our daughters a few years ago, the selection of a name was easy. We called *him* George, too.

George was almost fifty when I met him, and I was almost eighteen. We were drawn together by a common interest. I was interested in dating his daughter Barbara, and he was *very* interested in protecting her from a teenage goofball like me.

Given the circumstances, it took George and me a long time to become friends. But once we did, we were friends for the rest of his life. Come to think of it, we're *still* friends.

I wonder how the human mind decides which memories to keep in an accessible place, and which ones to tuck away in a seldom-used compartment. I wonder how it decides which picture to bring up when it's time to remember someone. However it happens, for years now the same image of George has appeared in my mind's eye. It's an image I treasure.

It's a sunny spring Sunday, and church has just let out. George is standing at the bottom of the church's front steps watching our children, his beloved grandchildren, scurry about in their Sunday best. He's wearing an old-fashioned suit with slightly baggy pleated pants that almost cover his wing-tip shoes, a neatly pressed shirt, and a wide necktie with a colorful geometric pattern—the kind of tie you find only in thrift stores these days.

He is wearing a totally delighted smile.

He is also wearing a hat.

The hat—felt in the winter, straw in the summer—is another thing I remember about George. In the twenties, thirties, and forties, men didn't feel fully dressed without a hat. Many never got over that feeling. Some men of that era *still* wear hats, even if it's just to sit on the porch and watch the world go by, or to walk out to the mailbox and get the evening paper. George was one of those men. He always wore a hat. When it was time to leave the house, he put on his hat. He didn't feel right without it.

Through the years I learned a great deal about George's background. His people were dry-goods merchants who left Europe to pursue their opportunities in the land of the free, eventually settling in Jackson, Tennessee. George's beloved older brother Sam succumbed to appendicitis when George was only five. Appendicitis is treated routinely now, but medical science hadn't progressed that far in the early twentieth century. The loss devastated the family, and George spent most of his early years trying to make up to his parents for the child they had lost. When George was in his teens his father died, forcing him to become the man of the house. It was a role he assumed with pride and determination, unaware of what he was giving up in exchange. He wore his nickname, Manny, as a badge of accomplishment, but a boy shouldn't have to become a little man. Boyhood should be savored. Once those years pass, they are gone forever.

Young George was bright as a dollar and motivated from within. He graduated from high school when he was sixteen. His heart's desire was to go to college and get an engineering degree. Wealthy uncles made deathbed promises to his father regarding young George's education, promises none of them kept. So, George went to work instead.

For the rest of his life, George would carry with him an oppressive feeling of total responsibility for his mother and his younger sister. He never complained about the weight on his shoulders or the heaviness in his heart, but they colored his existence. This was a terribly unfair burden to place on a young man, and it followed him forever like an oppressive cloud, far enough away to go unnoticed some of the time, but always close enough to block out some of life's precious sunshine.

George kept smiling, however, and kept on going.

George was a strong, athletic young man who stood at a well-built five-feet-nine. He loved football and Golden Glove boxing, and participated in both. His boxing years were a distant memory when I became part of his life, yet he had maintained his strength and was proud of it. I learned that in an interesting way one evening when I came to pick up his daughter for a date. He challenged me to a contest to see who could do the most one-arm push-ups. He won, of course, and he never let me forget it. After that, the challenge was tossed my way almost every time I showed up at his door, but like everything else in his life, he did it with a twinkle in his eye and a smile on his face.

Years later, when an aging Jack Palance did his one-arm push-ups at the Academy Awards ceremonies, I understood the manly pride which had driven him to demonstrate his strength that way. If George had been up there, he would have done the very same thing.

George was *strong*, but he wasn't *well*. He reached middle age long before the public had any real awareness of the difference between strength and fitness. Because of George's strength, we always assumed he was healthy. As it turned out, he was slowly dying inside.

The importance George placed on physical strength and manly acceptance of adversity led to an incident that was interesting, to say the least. I can laugh about it now, but I assure you it wasn't funny at the time.

One summer when Barbara and I were dating steadily, she went to camp for a couple of weeks. I missed her terribly, and on the Sunday afternoon when George was supposed to pick her up, I asked if I could go along. It was fine with him. He was glad to have the company.

We went by car. The trip took a little over an hour, but it seemed a lot longer. The car wasn't air conditioned, so we roared down the highway with all the windows rolled down.

Most of the time, my arm was half in, half out of the window. I was still wearing the long-sleeved dress shirt I had worn to church that morning, and I still remember how good the rushing wind felt as it puffed out my sleeve, causing my folded cuff to flap wildly.

Halfway to our destination, a bee flew into my wind-filled sleeve and began stinging my arm unmercifully. It wasn't a *large* bee, mind you, and the pain wasn't excruciating, but it *hurt*. Every time that bee stung me, it hurt that much more.

Consider my dilemma. Here I was, trapped in a car with my girlfriend's macho father, gritting my teeth while an ecstatic bee had the time of his life. Should I say something and expose myself to ridicule? Should I grit my teeth and bear it for the sake of my already suffering masculine image? Would I have any arm left when the ordeal was over?

I kept my mouth shut. Luckily, in a matter of minutes I cornered the tiny creature somewhere near my elbow and managed to get him.

He died with a smile on his face.

Years later, when I finally told George all about that incident, we had a good laugh together. As for my arm? Well, it healed nicely.

When I met him, George had been a traveling salesman for many grueling years. He left home every Monday morning, traveled his territory all week long, and returned home every Friday evening, exhausted. His weekends were spent doing the paperwork necessary to wrap up his efforts from the previous week, which left him with little time for life's pleasures. His life was structured to a fault. His routine was set in concrete.

Take, for example, the matter of the ten o'clock news. When he was home, George always watched the ten o'clock news. It marked the orderly conclusion of his day.

At Barbara's house, the family television set was in the living room. On Sunday evenings after vespers, she and I usually hung out at her place. Her family was extremely generous with their limited space. Years passed before I came to realize what an imposition my presence must have been, and what a sacrifice they made for their teenage children.

The sacrifice ended, however, at ten o'clock. Every Sunday night as the clock struck that hour, George padded into the living room wearing his pajamas, a plaid robe, slippers, and a determined look. He went straight to the television, switched it to his favorite channel, parked himself in "his" chair, and sat transfixed. Then, at precisely ten-thirty, he rose from his chair, turned the television set off, and left the room.

For that thirty minutes, Barbara and I might as well not have existed. We certainly didn't have to worry about him turning around!

George traveled the road long before the days of interstate highways and air-conditioned cars. He spent much of his life in hot, lonely hotel rooms, eating three meals a day in restaurants that knew nothing about fat-free or healthy cooking. By the time he knew what was happening, this demanding lifestyle was beginning to take its toll physically and emotionally. Raised to believe that providing for his family is a man's highest calling, George endured all this for a company in Detroit that made doors, windows, and other products for sale to the construction trade. Their products were first-class, and George took great pride in the results he achieved. Indeed, there are buildings all over the central South, recognizable buildings, where products George sold are still in constant use.

The products were good, but the policies of the company were often heartless and inhumane. Once, when things were going especially well for George, they arbitrarily divided his territory and gave part of it to someone else. At other times when things *weren't* going well, they turned the pressure up and demanded more than he could give. In both of these instances I saw his pain as he tried to carry on in spite of the way he was being treated.

Corporations can be incredibly cold and cruel. Employees aren't *people*, they are expendable assets. The only thing that matters is the bottom line. The end justifies the means. We knew and loved George as a man of honor, a man who tried hard, a man who believed in loyalty, one who simply *knew* that right would triumph in the end. But in Detroit, he was nothing more than a pin on a map. One fine day some faceless, dispassionate administrator pulled out the pin that bore George's name, and in a heartbeat, a lifetime of hard work and total loyalty was over, come to naught.

This happened early in my relationship with Barbara and her family, as did the chilling discovery that those pains George had recently started feeling in his chest were early signs of angina. George was never the same after that. His heart disease progressed at an incredible rate. He kept on smiling and kept on going, but both his faith in humanity and his physical well-being had suffered blows from which they would never fully recover. Yet he drew on his strength and faced life with a stubborn determination which proved to be both his friend and his foe. He endured incredible pain as his angina progressed, but he steadfastly refused to stop doing the things that brought on the pain. Life became a constant trial, both for this storm-tossed man and for those who loved him.

I don't remember exactly when George suffered the first of his five heart attacks, nor do I remember much about his time in the hospital or his recuperation. When something happens five times, the details tend to blend together. I do remember helping Barbara carry a tiny Christmas tree to his hospital room on one of those occasions, and there may have been a birthday spent there as well, or perhaps an Easter. His life became a series of hospitalizations, linked together by periods of constant apprehension. As in the case of his beloved brother Sam, George had the misfortune of being ill at a time when medical science had not yet found the key to his survival.

At one point, a ray of hope appeared in the form of a new

operation designed to enable the blood to bypass clogged arteries. His doctors tried it, but for him, the operation didn't succeed. The now-routine procedure was too experimental back then, and the damage caused by his heart attacks was too great. Hopefully, George's willingness to endure that operation contributed to the development of the improved procedures that now regularly bring relief. It's a sacrifice he gladly would have made if asked. He was that kind of man. No matter what life sent his way, he kept on smiling, and he kept on going.

The fifth heart attack brought an end to George's struggle more than twenty years ago, but I think about him now more than ever. God has blessed Barbara and me with grandchildren of our own, and our hearts still ache because George isn't around to enjoy them with us. There's no way to judge or evaluate a person's ability to love, but from my own experience, George loved his grandchildren just about as much as a man is capable of loving.

Put another way, he loved *his* grandchildren every bit as much as I love mine. I'm sorry that his years with his were so short.

All these recollections filled my heart during a recent Easter week as I prepared to speak to a group about the suffering of Jesus, my Savior, during his last days on earth.

Jesus, too, experienced death after five "attacks" on his heart.

The first attack came when Judas, one of his chosen twelve, handed Jesus over to his enemies in exchange for a few silver coins. This same Judas had sat at the table as part of the inner circle, and even though Jesus seemed to know what was going to happen and to understand that this was part of his own destiny, the agony of being cruelly betrayed by a so-called friend had to be much like that of a dagger being plunged directly into his heart.

But that had to pale into insignificance when compared with the pain inflicted on Jesus by Simon Peter. Jesus knew Judas for what he was. Peter, on the other hand, was a trusted companion, as close to the Master as anyone would ever be. Peter's attack on Jesus' heart had to bring with it a feeling of total abandonment. Few things have the power to hurt worse than that.

The people whom Jesus had come to save were the next to deliver a crushing blow. It wasn't too late. There was still time, and the people had a choice—one given them by Pilate. They held in their collective hands the power to end our Savior's agony, but they didn't exercise that power. Instead, they chose Barabbas.

The fourth attack came as Jesus was hanging on the cross. In full view of his suffering eyes, soldiers cast lots for the last of his earthly possessions. They didn't even have the good grace to wait until he had lost consciousness.

I can only imagine the hopelessness and utter despair that accompanied that sight.

The fifth attack on Jesus' heart came during his ninth hour on the cross, that moment when he reached the lowest point of his life. It was the moment—the *only* moment—when he thought his Father had abandoned him. "*Eli, Eli, lama sabachthani?*" was his plaintive cry. "My God, my God, why hast thou forsaken me?" (KJV).

After that, Jesus yielded up his spirit and allowed it to leave his earthly body. In that instant, the whole world changed. Those who believe in him still stand at the foot of the cross, where they and he learned the truth. God had not abandoned his Son, nor will God ever abandon us. Death is not an ending; it is only a beginning, a time when freedom comes at last and pain is felt no more.

There is one special memory of George that Barbara and I treasure, the one about the Bandit Box. Happily, we can return to that moment in a special way by watching it on a scratchy, faded old 8mm home movie.

George is sitting at the far end of the dining room table at his home, wearing pajamas and that ubiquitous plaid robe. Richard, our son, is in his lap. Richard is about eighteen months old. George has already suffered the fourth of his five attacks and his daily existence is filled with constant, debilitating pain. He no longer has the energy or the will to get dressed. His life is nearing its end, and even if his mind doesn't yet accept that fact, his heart must know it's true.

The Bandit Box is on the table in front of George and Richard.

The Bandit Box is a small black plastic box with a coin-shaped notch at one end of its top surface. When someone places a penny in that slot, it completes an electrical circuit, causing the box to do its thing. Richard's two-year-old brain doesn't know about electrical circuits. As far as he is concerned, the whole thing is an astounding feat of magic.

George helps Richard put a coin in the slot. As soon as he does so, the hinged lid of the box begins to rise upward in front of the coin. Richard's eyes widen expectantly.

Up and up the lid rises, ever so slowly, creating unimaginable excitement in young Richard's eyes. Then, in a flash, a small green hand reaches up out of the darkened box. The hand grabs the coin and jerks it inside just as the lid slams shut.

Although he has seen this happen a hundred times, Richard nearly jumps out of his skin. Then he convulses in laughter, totally surprised and delighted one more time.

Richard isn't the only one whose eyes widen in that film. George is every bit as expectant, and when Richard collapses in delight, George's laughter is just as real, and brings him just as much pleasure.

For that brief moment, his pain is forgotten. For that beloved moment, life is *good* again.

That film does, indeed, record a precious memory, a true glimpse of glory, a moment I go back to time and time again. The clouds of sorrow and pain are parted, and I see, if only for an instant, the indomitable spirit that God placed in George's body when he was born, the shining spirit that made him special, the happy, carefree spirit that we all loved so dearly. The sight of it always brings me great comfort. It reminds me that life is not the end. The undefeated human spirit, the *godlike* spirit, lives forever.

To this very day, my heart believes that somewhere, in a place I can only imagine, George's spirit flies free. My heart believes—it *knows*—that someday, at a time and place of God's own choosing, those who loved George will feel that spirit's presence once again.

COAL MINES, BABY CHICKS, AND HUMAN HEARTS

— · —

THE BABY CHICKS DIDN'T EVEN exist when our family arrived at the museum that morning. Well, they *existed*, but we couldn't see them. They were still inside the eggs.

The display was simple enough—a flat metal surface, warmed from above by heat lamps, protected on all sides by glass, completely covered with tiny flecks of some kind of grain, and populated only by a dozen or so eggs. The whole thing made up a kind of open-display incubator, where museum-goers could observe the miracle of birth, right there, while it happened.

But when would it happen? No one knew, no one could predict.

"Might as well watch grass grow," I said as we moved along.

Chicago's Museum of Science and Industry has undoubtedly kept pace with technical and scientific advancement in recent years, yet it couldn't be any better, or any more exciting, than it was when we first saw it two decades ago. It was a marvel of hands-on pleasure, fourteen acres of sheer delight. And to top it off, we happened along on a day when it was free!

We began our day in their incredibly realistic coal mine. We boarded a steel-and-mesh cage which carried us into the bowels of the earth. We plunged into darkness and emerged in a mine shaft, where we boarded a coal train for the ride even farther below. We learned all about the hard, hard life of the nameless, faceless men and women who risk physical and emotional destruction on a daily basis to keep one of our most important energy supplies flowing.

After that, we explored a giant-sized model of the human heart. We climbed through its chambers, poked our arms into ventricles and auricles, felt our way along veins and arteries, and listened to a disembodied voice sing the praises of this marvelous human machine.

Then, of course, there were the chicks.

As I said the first time we passed by that exhibit, we paused only for a second to see what it was about. We scarcely glanced at the familiar, motionless objects. Nothing was happening.

We moved along.

I have no idea why I chose to break away from our group and take a second look. Whatever the reason, I'm glad I did, because at the exact instant I arrived, one of the eggs wiggled ever so slightly.

I thought maybe someone had brushed against the display. I looked around. There was no one in sight.

I watched and waited to see whether the little egg would wiggle again, but it didn't, so I left. One can stare at a motionless egg for only so long.

The next exhibit we went to was, ironically, a display on childbirth, featuring models, diagrams, and photographs depicting the miracle of birth from conception to term. As interesting as it was, however, my mind kept wandering back to the baby chick.

After a while, I separated myself from our little group and hurried back to the incubator for the third time.

The egg was wiggling again when I returned. I decided to stick around and watch for a while.

Soon a tiny crack appeared in the egg's surface. Some of the other eggs were wiggling by then, but this little fellow was clearly in the lead, as far as the hatching process was concerned.

I cheered him on silently as he pecked away at the inside surface of his hard shell. I wondered what he must be feeling. My mind conjured up all sorts of possibilities. Was he scared? Was he anxious? Was he simply acting on instinct, blindly determined to leave his cramped quarters no matter what the alternative might be?

I wondered how he knew it was *time* for him to do what he was doing.

I wondered how he knew *what* to do, once he had realized that the time had come.

Soon the egg began to bulge at the point where it had first cracked. Other cracks appeared around that bulge, forming a minuscule spiderweb of fissures. The whole area was no bigger than a dime.

I watched, and I waited.

Two tiny pieces of shell fell away from the dime-sized spot, exposing a translucent membrane. Once that happened, other pieces of shell quickly followed. The warming lights were bright, and I could see, on the other side of the membrane, the pointed outline of a yellow beak punching away at the resilient surface. It wasn't long before the membrane broke, too. The yellow beak popped through the hole and extended itself out into totally unfamiliar territory.

The activity slowed after that, almost to a complete stop. I had no way of being certain, of course, but I imagined that the little fellow had paused to rest and was taking stock of his progress. Punching through that hard shell had to be hard work for one so young, one who wasn't even officially born yet. He deserved a rest, so I gave him my fatherly permission.

By then, you see, I was feeling rather like a member of the family.

I glanced nervously at my watch, then reluctantly abandoned my post to join the others of my family, who were already headed for the Nutrition Room.

I pretended to be interested, but my mind and my heart kept returning to the incubator and the struggling chick. Finally I decided to take my body back there, too.

A crowd had gathered around the little metal incubator table. Obviously something was happening. I shifted and squeezed my way forward until I could see over the heads of the children whose faces were almost pressed against the glass.

The hole in the egg was bigger at that point, and more than just a beak was hanging out. The chick's skinny little elbow had flopped out, but the rest of his head was still inside. He was pecking away at the circumference of the egg. The fissures now extended halfway around the once-smooth surface.

The tiny fellow seemed to know what needed to be done. He pulled his beak back inside and set about doing it.

My eyes stayed riveted to the egg as the chick tapped relentlessly away.

Every now and then the chick paused to take stock of his progress. When he did so, the tapping stopped and one of his little round eyes appeared in the ever-expanding hole. He would peek outside, make sure the world was still there, and then go back to work.

My son came to get me. The rest of my family was ready to explore another part of the museum, and they wanted me to come. I begged off. I was feeling very proud and very parental at that moment. There was no way I was going to abandon my new friend at a time like that.

My excitement must have been contagious, because my son went after the others, so *they* could see, *too.*

The little chick worked several minutes more, pecking and cutting in an even pattern along the circumference of the egg. Then it happened. It was so sudden that I almost gasped. The two sides of the egg folded neatly back, and the chick rolled out.

I wanted to applaud. I even looked around to see if anyone else's hands were poised and ready, but they weren't, so I didn't.

The chick landed on his side on the metal surface. He lay there in the equivalent of a fetal position for several moments. He was still shaped exactly like the egg from which he had just emerged. His legs and arms were so thin that he looked like a bundle of match sticks attached to a huge head. The surface of his body was covered with puckered skin. There were no discernible feathers. Patches of down were scattered about, but they were moist and matted. He looked as if he had been in a fight and had lost rather badly.

It was funny, but it was also sad, to see him lie there like that, completely motionless. One of the children nearest the glass turned in my direction. He had a pained look on his face.

"Is he dead?" the child asked gloomily.

"He's just taking a breather," I assured him. "I imagine he's pretty worn out."

Right about then, he began to move. His work was definitely not over. It had just begun. But first, with no one around to instruct him or model for him, he had to learn to stand.

It took forever.

The first thing he did was move his wings. He didn't *flap* them exactly, he just wiggled them back and forth, as if they were too stiff for him to actually do anything useful with them. Then he started doing the same thing with his fleshless legs.

He kicked out at the metal surface of the incubator again and again, pushing himself around in an ungainly half-circle. He got part of the way up, and then down he came, his head bumping against the floor. He did that repeatedly, without success. Then he stopped struggling and flopped back down in a motionless heap. Someone behind me gasped. We were *all* certain he was dead this time.

We were wrong. His clumsy dance quickly started up again. Everyone cheered.

The little chick stayed on his side for a while, circling and flopping crazily, trying his best, but meeting with absolutely no success. But he never gave up, and *finally*, through what appeared to be more of a happy accident than anything else, he found himself right side up.

He sat there, in a tight little upright crouch, and rested once again.

No one left the display.

His next goal was to pull his legs up under himself so they would be solidly beneath his body, instead of jutting crazily out to each side, which is what they did every time he tried to raise himself out of that crouch. This proved to be no easy trick. His toes were tightly curled and his feet were little balled-up wads, which made it next to impossible for him to balance himself. But he kept trying.

The dance had changed, but the result was the same. On and on he struggled, falling over, getting himself upright again, falling back over, each time breaking the hearts of all who were watching. His plight seemed quite hopeless for a while, and then the tide shifted in his favor. His toes straightened out. Almost immediately, he stood erect.

The applause was actually deafening.

There was no looking back for that little chick after that. There was nothing tentative about him anymore. He was as proud of himself as he could be—we could tell by the way he strutted and preened. He marched about, examining his world, demonstrating the confident air of one who had been walking like that for years.

I *promise* you, there was an instant when the little chick paused and glanced our way. Maybe it was wishful thinking on my part, but it even seemed as if he nodded in our direction, acknowledging our presence, thanking us for our support. Then he turned away and wandered over to one of the other eggs. He peered down at the small hole that had appeared in its surface, cocked his head quizzically, then walked on by and headed for the feed bowl, where he buried his beak in a delectable pile of grain.

The show was over. One by one, the spectators began to wander away. A new group ambled over to witness the next arrival. The rest of my family trudged off, but I stayed a few minutes longer, caught up in the wonder of it all.

How did that little chick know it was time for him to come out into the world?

How did he know he was supposed to stand up, once he got here?

What made him think he *could* stand on his own two feet? Once he was upright, how did he know what to do next? How did he know to head straight for the food bowl? He was alone at the moment of his birth. No mother was there to teach him, no father was present to lend a hand, there weren't even any other chicks to set an example. Yet somehow he knew. He came into this world knowing everything he needed to know in order to survive.

Life is amazing, I thought as I stood there. Absolutely amazing. Birth, death, and everything in between is a miracle. Nothing less.

I hurried off to catch up with the rest of my family.

I didn't see that little chick again. We passed by the incubator a couple of hours later on the way out, and I glanced over that way as we passed, but by then the glass box with the metal floor was crawling with brightly feathered creatures. There was no way to tell one from another. Yet the memory of that little yellow fellow stayed with me, and when I got on my knees that night, I thanked God for letting me see what I had seen.

Life is a miracle. *New* life may be the greatest miracle of them all.

Fried-Egg Sandwiches and Other Comforts of Home

— • —

My eyes actually popped open for the final time at 3:30, but another half hour lumbered by before I admitted that I was awake. The last thing I wanted that early in the morning was to give up on the possibility of sleep.

I slipped out of bed as quietly as possible so as not to disturb Barbara, donned my robe and slippers, and headed for the den.

I flopped down on a chair in the den and picked up a book, but my eyes were too scratchy to read. They felt like huge, sand-covered globes. I turned on the television, but the only available channels were offering loud, obnoxious people asking for money. Even if there *had* been something to watch, my attention span was nonexistent.

I turned off the television and sat there.

After a while I wandered out to the side porch to look at the moon. It was bright and full, the exact opposite of the way I felt. I stared at it a few seconds, then returned indoors. I stood in the middle of the kitchen feeling helpless, grumpy, aggravated, and half-awake. I had no idea what to do with myself.

That's when I remembered the old family remedy for insomnia. My father had taught it to me years earlier. *His* father had taught *him*, and so on back through the generations to the beginning of time, or at least to the invention of bread.

29

Milk toast.

That was the ticket. Milk toast!

Even the *idea* made me feel better.

Milk toast is warm, soothing, kind to the stomach, and altogether agreeable. It does just what it is supposed to do, nothing more, nothing less. It fills the void in your stomach and then lies there, silently humming a gentle lullaby. And it's easy to make. You take two slices of white bread, toast them, butter them on one side, place them in a flat, shallow bowl, heat some milk, and pour it on top.

Milk toast is one of the few things a man can fix without prior training, and it's probably the *only* thing a man can fix without having to be fully awake.

Thirty minutes after giving birth to the idea, my stomach was pleasantly full, my psyche was comforted, my eyes were closed, and I was well on the way back to sleep.

The fact that a major family problem had been resolved in the process didn't become apparent until the next morning.

The problem was one of sibling rivalry.

When I first started writing inspirational stories, I called each of my three children to ask for permission to use their names. These stories are all true, and many involve members of my family in one way or another. I didn't want to write about any particular child unless the child in question was comfortable with the idea.

I began by calling Richard, the youngest of the three. I told him I wanted to put together a book. His reaction pleased me, and surprised me a bit, too.

"That's a great idea, Dad," he exclaimed. "Go for it. And be sure to include The Pancake Man. It's my all-time favorite!"

I was delighted to know he had a favorite.

"In fact, I think you ought to *call* the book *The Pancake Man*," he continued.

I wasn't expecting such a suggestion, and to tell you the truth, I was a bit taken aback. The title of a book is crucial to its success; I just wasn't sure that title would work.

The fact that the book has succeeded as *The Pancake Man and Friends* shows how little I know about titles.

A year later, I put together another collection, which my publisher and I titled *Second Helpings: More Stories from the Pancake Man*. That book's title seemed to flow naturally from the first book's title, but when the publisher ordered a third book, I was at a loss. I hadn't given it any thought, and there was no obvious choice.

Lindy, the younger of my two daughters, came to my rescue.

Lindy knew that her brother had named the first book, and she was determined to name one herself. She had never said a word about it to me, or to anyone else, but apparently her brain had been working on it all along.

One December day, when she was home from college for Christmas, she made her move.

I was sitting at our breakfast table, reading the morning paper. Lindy pulled up a chair and plopped herself down across from me.

"I've got a title for your next book," she chirped gaily.

I put down my paper.

"You do?"

I was pleasantly surprised.

"Yeah!" Lindy has a naturally happy voice. She can fill a room with joy when she speaks, and she was obviously happy with herself at that moment.

"What is it?" I asked.

"Fried-egg sandwiches and other comforts of home!"

I liked it immediately.

"How'd you come up with *that*?" I asked.

Lindy smiled warmly. "Richard remembers pancakes. Well, *I* remember fried-egg sandwiches!"

"You do?"

"Sure! When I was a teenager, sometimes I would come home late at night, all upset and needing to talk. No matter how late it was, Mama would always sit up and listen, and you would always make me a fried-egg sandwich!"

I have never been paid a nicer compliment.

Well, when Lindy's older sister Barby heard about Lindy's plan, she immediately decided, and publicly declared, that *she* was going to name the *next* book.

When I reported that development to Lindy, she laughed out loud.

"Barby hasn't got a prayer!"

I was puzzled. "Why not?"

"What's she gonna call it?" she asked.

"Well . . ."

"Let's face it, Dad. Once pancakes and fried-egg sandwiches are out of the way, you're *done* in the kitchen. There's nothing left to choose from." She chortled. "Naming a book after boiled water doesn't seem like a good idea."

Lindy had a point, but after my sleepless night, I had a solution. Now, all I have to do is fix Barby some milk toast and hope she takes the hint.

I'm glad fried-egg sandwiches were a comfort food for Lindy. I'm glad to know she felt safe and welcome when she came home late at night. I'm glad she found her mother so easy to talk to. I'm glad she found our kitchen table a safe haven, where she could deal with things that mattered.

A child wanting to talk, a mother willing to listen, a father ready to prepare a simple sandwich, and a table where all three can sit down together. Put them together, and you have a meaningful memory for all concerned.

That's the way her mother and I had always hoped it would be.

Memorable family moments are often centered around a table. Plain or fancy, crowded or not, the table is a place of comfort, a place where people who love one another can gather together to talk, laugh, cry, remember the past, and make plans for the future.

The family table is a common denominator, around which all kinds of people gather. It's an equalizer, bringing parents and children to the same level, where they can be face-to-face and heart-to-heart. It's an enabler, where busy people pause and share their experience before getting back on the fast-moving train we call life. For most modern families, it's probably the only place where everyone gathers at one time on any regular basis. It ought to be the most well-loved, most fondly remembered place in any home.

That lofty goal can be reached, but only through effort. It doesn't happen by accident. That's why it thrilled me so to hear that Lindy had such positive memories of her late evening sessions with her mom and me, and the warm reassurance of fried-egg sandwiches served at our table.

Barbara and I still have the table we bought when we married thirty-two years ago. It's a tiny thing made of wood-grain Formica, with spindly metal legs at each corner. It was the very first piece of furniture in our very first apartment, and although it hasn't been in use for years, there's no way either of us would part with it. We faced each other across that table and planned our life together. We made a place for Barby, then for Lindy, and finally for Richard. As the family grew, so did the love we shared and the laughter we experienced during our times together.

That table was a table of love. It's a symbol of love even now. It's gathering dust, but it isn't losing its importance.

Another table comes to mind when I think about home, a table that holds no pleasant memories, but one that taught me something about courage and determination.

It was a cumbersome structure made of wrought iron and steel. With several other equally ugly tables, it sat on the styleless slab of concrete that surrounded the pool at a second-rate motel in a declining part of Nashville. Several remarkably uncomfortable, partially rusted chairs were usually pulled up around it, and a badly soiled umbrella always hung askew atop its supporting pole.

That cumbersome piece of rusted metal might have been bulky, ugly, and useless most of the time, but during the summer of 1960, it was a banquet table of the first order. Sunday after Sunday, it groaned under the weight of mounds of food—meats, vegetables, salads, and breads—all prepared on a two-burner ministove in the cramped kitchenette that adjoined room number four, a few steps away from the terrace.

Those were miserable, desperate, agonizing times.

Each Sunday for several endless months I joined my parents and two of my siblings around that table for the traditional midday meal. Barbara came when she could, thank goodness; she was the only positive thing in my life at that time. Five members of my family, myself included, were living in the cramped confines of one nondescript room at that motel—not because we wanted to, but because there was no other place for us to go. The bottom had fallen out for my father. Everything was gone—house, cars, most of our furnishings—everything. Our family had no home, no money, no prospects, and no realistic hope.

But we had dinner every Sunday around that table.

It was awkward and uncomfortable, to say the least. I, for one, remember feeling extremely conspicuous. None of the other guests could possibly have known what was going on, but that didn't help. They stared at us, and it hurt. To them we weren't *people*; we were objects of pity.

They *had* to stare. No doubt we presented a bizarre sight as we clung desperately to our family tradition under extremely difficult circumstances. We smiled weakly at one another, if we smiled at all, and made small talk to avoid touching on anything real. We pretended to have a good time, mostly for the sake of one another's feelings. We carried on as if everything were okay, even though it clearly wasn't.

Those were unbelievably painful days. It hurts to remember them even now, all these years later.

That wrought-iron table stands out in my memory. It is, to me, a symbol of determination and a stubborn unwillingness to surrender to the vicissitudes of life. I will always admire the courage my mother showed during that awkward situation. She did her best to keep the fractured remains of her family from growing even farther apart. She expressed love the only way she ever knew how, by cooking and serving a delicious meal.

Fortunately for me, there was another table in my life at that time. Barbara and I weren't yet married, but we loved each other deeply. I had nowhere else to go, so her home became my second home that summer.

I'm sure I drove her parents to distraction much of the time, hanging around their house as much as I did, but they never once showed it. With remarkable patience and understanding, they cut me all the slack I needed. Even at mealtime—make that *especially* at mealtime—I felt welcome. There was always an extra plate, plenty of food, and, most important, an atmosphere of love. And late at night, when *I* was the one who needed to talk, the coffee was always hot, there was always something in the oven, and genuine compassion and concern were always available for the asking.

That table saved my sanity.

* * *

There came a time in his life when Jesus needed a place to gather his friends. He needed to tell them that for him, the end was near. He needed to express his love by making a covenant with each of them, and with us, a covenant that would last forever.

He chose a table.

It was the time of the Passover feast, a lasting memorial to the night when the angel of death passed over the houses of the Israelites living in Egypt, the houses whose doorways were marked with the blood of a lamb.

Jesus was in Jerusalem, and so were his disciples. They gathered in an upper room, sat around a table, and took that sacred meal together, just as their forefathers had done for generations.

What was it like around that table? Was there laughter? That's what usually happens when people who like each other come together. Was love present? Wherever Jesus went, love was always there. Courage, determination, patience, acceptance—they were there, too. Jesus was dining with one who would betray him, and he knew it. This would be his last Passover meal—he knew that, too. But more important, he knew it was the right place and the right time.

Jesus took bread and broke it. In the process, he changed the world. But isn't it interesting that it all began where so many changes begin, at a simple table, spread with good food, surrounded by good people, and filled to the brim with love.

Angels No Longer Unaware

— ∎ —

ON THE MORNING OF AUGUST 20, 1956, I WAS decked out in all the appropriate gear, sweating like a pig in the morning sun, trying my best to make my high school football team.

Passing drills had just begun. I was standing in line, awaiting my turn. My assignment was to run straight ahead fifteen yards, then cut toward the sideline at full tilt. Hopefully, the ball and I would arrive at the same spot near the sideline at the same time.

The defensive back's assignment was to do whatever was necessary to keep me from catching the ball.

At the proper time, I followed the coaches' instructions to the letter. I covered the fifteen yards as fast as I could, then made a sharp outward turn. When I arrived at the designated spot, the ball was coming right at me.

My arms reached upward. The ball and the defensive back arrived at exactly the same instant. The ball hit my hands. The defensive back hit my gut. The ball bounced away harmlessly. I crumpled to the ground, doubled up in severe pain.

I knew better than to show fear or pain on the practice field. Young athletes just don't do that, especially when they haven't yet earned a spot on the team. So I climbed to my feet as quickly as I could and limped back to my place in the line.

It's okay to limp. Limping shows your willingness to

carry on in spite of your pain. I hoped the coaches were appropriately impressed with my display of courage.

The pain subsided after a while. My teammates and I finished morning practice, had lunch, and returned for the afternoon session. I didn't know at the time how much damage had been done. I had no idea I was bleeding inside.

The afternoon practice session began with wind sprints, during which we ran up and down the steep hill in front of our school. I can only imagine how much that must have accelerated the unseen bleeding that was slowly but surely draining my life away.

There was a party that night, a cookout at a local church. I went with friends, but we parted company early in the evening. I wasn't feeling very well. My stomach hurt. For some reason, I didn't connect that to the blow I had received earlier in the day. Instead, I blamed it on the Boston baked beans I had wolfed down at the party.

It was years after that before I ever wanted another taste of Boston baked beans.

I managed to get to sleep that night, but I didn't stay asleep very long. The nagging, growing, throbbing ache in my abdomen got worse and worse as the night progressed.

Some time after midnight, I left my upstairs bedroom and went downstairs. My intention was to rummage around in the kitchen cabinets to see if I could find something to ease the pain. By that time, the entire middle of my body was pulsating with steady spasms.

I never made it to the kitchen. I collapsed in a heap on the den sofa and clutched a small foam-rubber pillow to my stomach. I was unable to go anywhere else, or even stand up. The pain was too great. I lay there until four in the morning, with the pain increasing by the minute. All I could do was clench my teeth and groan.

It was years after *that* before I could stand the smell of foam rubber.

My mother finally heard my cries and came downstairs to see what was wrong. I don't know what I told her, but I remember very well what I was feeling. I felt as if someone were cutting me in half with a chain saw.

My father was out of town. My mother called Dr. Norman Cassell, a neighbor, who was doing his pediatric residency at Vanderbilt. He came to our house immediately, took one look at me, lifted me bodily, threw me over his shoulder, and carried me to his car. He told my mother there wasn't time to wait for an ambulance.

I was twice Dr. Cassell's size at the time, and he still can't figure out how he managed to lift me up and throw me over his shoulder. Personally, I think he had some help from above.

Dr. Cassell drove me to the hospital. The doctors who were present in the emergency room wanted to do some tests. Dr. Cassell wouldn't let them waste that time. Instead, he grabbed a phone, called a surgeon he knew, and told him to rush to the hospital.

I was on the operating table in a matter of minutes.

The surgeon told me later that when he first drew the scalpel across my distended midsection, blood spurted out with such force that it sprayed the ceiling of the operating room. Practically all my blood had poured out into my peritoneal cavity, filling it like a balloon.

If Dr. Cassell hadn't taken command, I certainly would have died.

Dr. Cassell still practices pediatrics in Nashville. He has been a trusted friend, mentor, and physician to all three of our children. Every time I see him, we laugh about that early morning in 1956, when he did the impossible, with God's help.

When the surgery was over, my mother was told I wasn't likely to survive. I had lost too much blood.

I drifted in and out for the next two days, but was

never fully conscious. If I experienced a near-death encounter during that time, I have no recollection of it. I have little memory of anything, however, except for some bizarre, irrational nightmares about a world made entirely of foam rubber, where everything tasted like Boston baked beans.

I finally drifted into consciousness on the morning of the third day.

I can still see the comforting, loving sight that greeted me when I regained consciousness after the operation. I was still alive, yet I was looking into the face of an angel.

The angel was a woman called Sister Mary Antoinette.

Sister Antoinette was sitting by my bed, holding my hand. A graceful white cloth covered her head in the manner of her order. Only her face was visible, and it was very close to mine, filling my entire field of vision. She was smiling ever so slightly. There was a calmness about her, a sense of unflappable peace.

Her skin was flawless and luminescent, almost ivory in color. But it's her eyes I remember best. I can't even begin to describe them. They were clear, deep, vibrant, and intensely alive. She didn't just *look* at me, she reached out to me from deep within her soul.

Sister Antoinette didn't seem at all surprised that I had awakened at that precise moment, when she was the only person in my room. In fact, it seemed as though she had expected it to happen.

Her eyes remained fixed on mine. She placed her hand first on my brow, then on my cheek. Her touch was warm and gentle. It was also powerful. I could literally feel her energy flowing into my soul.

"We've been praying for you," she said.

Her voice was soft and reassuring. It brought me peace.

She looked away, moving only her eyes. I followed her

gaze to a tiny silver medallion pinned to the sleeve of my hospital gown.

"What's that?" I asked, managing only a whisper.

"It's a Miraculous Medal."

She lifted the medallion so that I could see it better.

"I pinned it on you in the emergency room. It's been with you all along."

"What's it for?" I asked. My Protestant upbringing hadn't introduced me to such things.

"It's our way of telling God how much we love you and how much we care. It's our way of asking God to hold your hand when we can't be there. It's our way of asking God to perform a miracle if one is needed."

I was instantly aware that God had answered her prayer. I was alive because God *wanted* me alive.

Sister Antoinette came to see me every day during my stay in the hospital, but we were never alone again. Our visits were on a much different level after that. She was pleasant company, and we even prayed together, but it was different.

I wore that Miraculous Medal on a chain around my neck for years, continually drawing comfort from its presence. I still have it. I also had a small sign printed which read "Remember the 20th." I put it in a frame and placed it on my bedside table to remind me of the day I was supposed to die, and to remind me of the presence of two of God's angels in my life. I still have that sign, too.

Time magazine once published a poll which determined that two-thirds of all Americans believe in the existence of angels. I am part of that majority.

Sister Mary Antoinette and Norman Cassell were the first angels I *remember* in my life, but there may have been others before them. Certainly they weren't the last. Angels have appeared in my life several times since then, always when they were most needed.

Does God send angels in the form of human beings, as I believe he does?

Chapter 13, verse 2 of the Letter to the Hebrews seems to say so quite clearly:

Do not neglect to show hospitality to strangers,
for thereby some have entertained angels unaware. (RSV)

Even more compelling is the story of the birth of Samson, found in chapter 13 of the Book of Judges (NKJ).

In that chapter we are introduced to the woman who eventually will give birth to Samson. But when we meet her she is barren. She has been unable to bear children. We can only imagine the anguish this must have caused both her and her husband, a man named Manoah.

But this will soon change.

And the Angel of the LORD appeared to the woman and said to her, "Indeed now, you are barren and have borne no children, but you shall conceive and bear a son." (13:3)

When the angel had finished telling her what she needed to do, the woman hurried to Manoah to tell him the news:

"A Man of God came to me, and His countenance was like the countenance of the Angel of God." (13:6)

God had sent his angel. The scripture is clear on that. But the woman to whom he was sent, when she *looked* upon the angel, saw instead a Man of God.

Once the woman's husband had heard all that his wife had to say, he prayed to the Lord:

"O my Lord, please let the Man of God whom You sent
come to us again." (13:8)

And God listened to the voice of Manoah, and the Angel
of God came to the woman again as she was sitting in the
field. (13:9)

Once again the woman was alone when the angel
appeared to her. Once again she hurried to tell Manoah
what had happened. This time, however, Manoah went
back to that spot with her, so he could see for himself.

Manoah spoke to the angel who had come in the form
of a man, and even invited him to stay and join them at
their table,

(For Manoah did not know He was the Angel of the
LORD.) (13:16c)

So you see, the Bible says it's true, and I believe it. I
believe that God can, indeed, infuse his children with his
Spirit and use them as angels. Indeed, I believe God has
used *me* as an angel in the lives of other people.

Let me relate the most compelling of such incidents.

During the last few years I have found myself in the
presence of men who, like myself, have suffered major
reversals in their lives and are struggling with depression
and emotional turmoil. I have felt firsthand the painful
loneliness and isolation which all too often comes with a
life-changing crisis. I know how important it is to be with
someone who cares, someone who will listen and not be
judgmental, someone who *has been there* and can shed
some light on the tortured path.

An acquaintance of mine was in just such a situation.
He was about my age, perhaps somewhat younger. Like
me, he was a trial lawyer, which, as I know all too well, is
a profession tailor-made for crises.

This man and I had never been close friends. The opportunity to develop a genuine friendship had never arisen. Our paths had crossed many times, however, and our meetings had always been cordial and pleasant. I liked him. When I learned of his distress, I wanted to help.

His time of crisis came a couple of years after mine, and I offered to share some of my experience.

We started meeting on a regular basis, usually for breakfast. I began to learn more about his situation. Among other problems, his marriage was in serious trouble. His most pressing concern was how to keep it from disintegrating.

My friend never found a solution to that dilemma. His wife left him soon after we started meeting. His spirit was crushed. His pain was enormous. To make matters worse, he lived in fear that he wouldn't be able to maintain a relationship with his two adorable daughters.

The weeks that followed his wife's departure were filled with apprehension, accusations, and acrimony. Not all of his decisions during that time were wise, and not all of his actions were prudent or productive. In other words, he was human. He wanted his wife back, and in his own aggressive way, he did what he could to keep her from permanently severing their ties. Saving his marriage and being a full-time father to his children was the most important thing in his life. The thought of doing otherwise was too painful to even think about, much less address.

His situation was desperate, and there was nothing I could do to provide the kind of help he wanted. I found myself being emotionally drained by our meetings. He needed more help than I could give.

I stopped meeting with him.

Weeks passed, then months. Although I lost track of time, I began to feel guilty. I still cared about him and wanted to know how he was, but I feared being drawn into his emotional vortex once again. So I continued to keep my distance, and the feeling of guilt continued to grow.

My friend's office was in a renovated house very near my writing studio. I drove past it every day. Sometimes I did so with a twinge of guilt; other times I wasn't even aware it was there. But I never bothered to stop.

One day, when my friend wasn't on my mind at all, I was on my way to do something I thought was important. I was glad to be alive, and was totally preoccupied with my own needs and my own feelings.

As it turned out, I had to drive right past his office, and I glanced idly in that direction. The building looked exactly the same as it had always looked. There was nothing remarkable about it. There was no hint of the turbulence that was going on inside.

I promised myself that I would give him a call sometime soon.

To my complete surprise, my car turned into his drive and started to accelerate.

No, I didn't take my hands off the wheel, and I didn't turn control of the car over to some unseen power or presence. I was fully aware of what was happening the whole time. But I made no conscious decision to alter my course; of that I am absolutely certain. I was completely shocked when my car came to a stop at my friend's backdoor.

My friend's sister was standing in the doorway. There was a troubled look on her face. She didn't ask why I was there.

"He needs you," is all she said.

She stepped aside and let me in. As we climbed the stairs together, she kept talking.

"He was looking out the window. When he saw you turn in, he turned to me and said, 'Thank God. My angel is here.' "

She led me to his office. He was sitting behind his desk. His face was red, his eyes were swollen, and tears were rolling down his cheeks. In spite of it all, he was smiling.

His first words confirmed what I already knew.

"You know who sent you, don't you?" he asked.

"He didn't just send me," I answered with a smile. "He *brought* me."

My friend didn't press for an explanation. We both understood what had happened.

I spent more than an hour in my friend's office that day. I listened to what he had to tell me, but rarely offered a response. There wasn't anything I *could* say that would change things. He had just received the papers he had been dreading all along, the ones he had hoped would never come, the ones that would begin the final, painful process of divorce. It was the beginning of the end of his family, or so it seemed at the time.

He told me it was the worst day of his life. I believed him.

Was that horrible day made more bearable for my friend because I was there? I have to believe it was, because it was God who sent me. God cares when his children are in pain. He promised to send a comforter, the Holy Spirit. I believe God sometimes sends that spirit in the form of another human being.

I left my friend's office filled to overflowing with gratitude, wonder, and amazement at the way God had worked in both our lives. He had used a man who had known sorrow and was acquainted with grief to reach out to another man in crisis.

On that day, I was privileged to be one of God's angels. Both my friend and I were aware of it and convinced of it. We both believed that I had followed a path not of my own making or design, but one selected by God for his own purpose, to further God's kingdom on earth.

The Butter Eater from Al Khobar

— • —

I WAS SUPPOSED TO MEET MR. NAZER at the Nashville airport. I made certain I wasn't late. Since I had no idea what he looked like, I wanted to be there when the passengers started coming off of the morning plane from Houston.

The plan was simple, but the schedule was tight. I would pick him up, take him to lunch, whisk him off to our very important meeting, and then get him back to the airport in time to catch an evening flight to Riyadh, Saudi Arabia. He wouldn't be in Nashville very long, but it was the best he could do. He didn't come to the United States often, and he didn't plan to return any time soon. If I wanted his expertise, I had to grab him when I could.

This meeting was very important to me and my law partners. We would have gone to almost any length to get the benefit of his knowledge.

As the passengers began to deplane, I studied each of them in turn, looking for someone who fit the image I had projected of this stranger from a foreign land. I had pictured him as being tall, bearded, olive-skinned, and serious. He might be wearing a robe instead of a suit; maybe even one of those things Saudi men wind around their heads to protect themselves from the blazing desert sun. All that was pure speculation, of course. All I really knew was that he was a highly regarded, very expensive, very powerful lawyer from the Middle East, and I assumed he would look the part.

47

Well, he didn't. I very nearly missed him completely. Fortunately, *he* found *me*!

Mr. Nazer turned out to be diminutive, rather than tall; portly rather than lean; pink-skinned rather than olive; and with sparse strands of gray hair sprouting from his head rather than a turban. He had a twinkling smile, a gleam in his eye, and a genuinely friendly demeanor. And he wasn't as portly as he first appeared. Much of his bulk resulted from the three layers of clothing he was wearing. He liked to travel light, and he hated to check baggage, so he just *wore* everything he thought he might need.

At the time of his visit, my law firm was involved in a very complex lawsuit arising out of a fire that had taken place in Saudi Arabia. A Tennessee construction company had built an apartment complex to house expatriate medical personnel and staff at the King Faisal Specialist Hospital in Riyadh. The hospital was being built by the king for which it was named, as a model of excellence for the world.

It ended up being a *memorial* to him after his untimely assassination.

When the hospital was almost finished, the Saudis suddenly realized that housing was needed in a hurry, otherwise there would be no place for hospital personnel to live.

Unfortunately, no housing had been planned.

With everyone's full knowledge, the Tennessee construction company suggested using a design and materials that were more appropriate to a humid climate than to the dry desert heat. The downside was that it would be flammable. The upside was that it would be ready on time. It was the only solution offered, and nobody had any better ideas, so the construction company was given the go-ahead. They built it. It burned. All of a sudden, everyone acted surprised.

The construction company was sued. I was hired to

defend them. I needed to know as much as I possibly could about Saudi Arabian law.

Enter Mr. Nazer.

Once he found me, we exchanged greetings, negotiated our way through the crowded airport, found my car, and headed for town.

Our first stop was a very nice restaurant. I wanted to make a good impression.

While we were waiting for our food, the waiter brought a small silver bowl to the table. The bowl was filled with ice, on which sat a pile of butter patties. As soon as the waiter put it down, Mr. Nazer pulled the bowl over to his place at the table, picked up his fork, and proceeded to eat every single one of the butter patties, one at a time, smiling all the while.

I was dying to ask, but I held my tongue, and he offered no explanation whatever.

Once he had finished his bowl of butter and I had recovered my composure, he began to talk.

His full name, he told me, was Ismail S. Nazer. He was a native of Palestine and now lived in Al Khobar, Saudi Arabia. Al Khobar is located on the Persian Gulf, next to a vast desert, about two hundred fifty miles from the Saudi capital of Riyadh.

He was educated at King's College, London, and was admitted to practice as a member of the Inner Temple Bar, Inns of Court, Queen's Bench. As such, he was a licensed Barrister-at-Law, entitled to practice his profession in all of the courts of the United Kingdom.

Life had taken him far afield from the Queen's Bench and Fleet Street, however. He practiced law in the kingdom of Saudi Arabia, and had offices and clients in Al Khobar and Riyadh in Saudi Arabia, and in New York, Los Angeles, and Houston in the USA.

Mr. Nazer told me with unabashed pride that he

occupied a rather unique place in the history of Saudi jurisprudence. He had begun practicing law there in 1952, but it wasn't until 1960 that the king recognized the necessity of licensing lawyers in that country. Ismail S. Nazer was issued law license number five. The holders of licenses one through four had long since died, which made him a senior member of his profession in that oil-rich kingdom.

I was impressed. He was obviously glad.

After lunch, we proceeded to my office, where we took over a conference room and went to work. We were joined that afternoon by two other lawyers who represented codefendants and wanted to hear what our visitor from the East had to say. We had a court reporter present so that we could preserve our conversation.

Actually, there wasn't a lot of "conversation" around that table that afternoon. I *did* ask questions from time to time, just to keep things going, but for the most part, Mr. Nazer simply held court. He knew what we wanted—a crash course on Saudi Arabian jurisprudence—and he knew how to give it to us.

He began by telling us that Saudi law is God's law, and that the most pure representation of that law is found in the Koran, which is literally God's word. There is no such thing as different versions of the Koran; there is only the original. Where it speaks, it does so with absolute, unyielding authority.

Unfortunately, the Koran doesn't "speak" concerning many of the problems that tend to arise in a modern society, so something more is required.

Mr. Nazer explained that the *second* level of authority is the prophet Muhammad. When a problem isn't specifically addressed in the Koran, one turns first to Muhammad's *interpretations* of the Koran, then to his other writings dealing with life's problems, and then to the examples he set during his lifetime. If no answer is found in those, one may then turn to the lesser prophets, including Jesus Christ.

According to him, if one has to search beyond the lives and teachings of the lesser prophets, things become a bit fuzzy.

The next level of authority is what they call the Old Authorities, which consists of the collected rules and regulations of the Shari'a judges. These prior pronouncements aren't binding on the *present* Shari'a judges, however—not even the ones they wrote themselves. A Shari'a judge can do whatever he wants to do, and he *can't* be wrong, because however far removed it may be, his authority comes directly from God.

Mr. Nazer described the system as "firm, but fair." It sounded more like "tough luck, buddy" to me.

I asked him what he meant by "firm but fair."

"The whole system is really quite dependable," he suggested. "If you do something wrong and are caught, you *will* be punished. And you know *exactly* what that punishment is going to be."

"Can you give me an example?"

He answered in his even, businesslike voice:

"If you take something that belongs to another, you will go to prison. The only variable is the length of time, but that doesn't matter much anyway. Even the prospect of a *short* stay in a Saudi prison is enough to make a man think twice." He smiled. "Of course, if you enter a man's *sanctity* when you take his property, it's a different story entirely."

"His sanctity?" I thought I knew what he was driving at, but I wanted to be certain.

"Entering his sanctity means taking his property from his person or from his place. If you do *that*, the punishment is the removal of your primary hand in public."

I gulped. "They cut off your hand in public?"

"I've seen it done," he assured me. "It's really quite effective."

"I'll bet!"

His smile broadened. He sensed my discomfort and continued:

"You must understand that the public impact of punishment is quite important in my country. The people need to see justice in action. It will remind them that there may be similar consequences for their own misconduct. Thus the public removal of a hand, coupled with the day-to-day presence of this handless person in the stream of society, serve as a constant reminder of the wages of crime."

I was, indeed, uneasy, but one of the other lawyers in the room was even *more* uncomfortable. It seems that many years ago this lawyer had lost his thumb, and as Mr. Nazer's account unfolded, he had become very self-conscious and had tried to hide his deformity. The rest of us didn't know that until he finally held up the thumbless hand for all to see.

"I didn't do a thing," he said, looking at Mr. Nazer and smiling sheepishly. "It was a lawnmower accident! I swear!"

We all laughed.

"Westerners have a difficult time with these concepts," Mr. Nazer continued, understating the obvious. "I talked recently with an American supervisor who had charge of a construction crew working in my country. One of his workmen had somehow managed to make some whiskey, which is strictly forbidden. The local police took the *supervisor* into custody, not the workman. The next day, the supervisor was brought before the Shari'a judge, who explained what the workman had done. The judge told the supervisor that he would be held in jail until his people located the individual involved and escorted him out of the country. The supervisor thought he'd been treated unfairly, but had he really? *My* people weren't going to investigate. *They* weren't going to punish. And why should they? That was *his* responsibility, as supervisor."

"I understand," I muttered, trying to be cordial without specifically agreeing. Yet I didn't disagree, either. The whole thing had an air of practical effectiveness about it.

"Preventing others from committing criminal acts is very important in my country," he went on. "And the *most* effective deterrent is the practice of stoning."

"Stoning?" I asked incredulously. "You mean they still *do* that?"

"Indeed they do," he admitted. He seemed remarkably matter-of-fact about it, as if it were nothing special to him.

"How? Why? Where?" I stammered in disbelief.

"First, let me tell you why," he began calmly. "You have to go back to the fundamental position that the Koran can't be wrong, since it's the verbatim word of God. So there isn't any contrary opinion or second guessing about stoning in Saudi Arabia. It is fully accepted because God has decreed that it be done, and God is incapable of a wrong act. Thus, just as in the case of the removal of a hand for certain kinds of thefts, if the judge finds that a crime punishable by stoning has been committed, then stoning is the punishment. No choices, no options, and for all practical purposes, no ethical struggle or guilt. If the deed has been done, that's it."

"What kind of crimes are punishable by stoning?" I asked.

"Stoning is reserved for crimes which involve a morally bad decision," he answered. "Murder with malice, rape, sodomy, bestiality, maybe even homosexuality. That hasn't been tested yet, but in Saudi Arabia, no one admits to being homosexual. The risk is far too great."

"Have you ever actually *seen* a stoning?"

"In a manner of speaking, yes."

"What does *that* mean?"

"To understand, you need to know how and why it is done," he explained. "It takes place in the courtyard of a mosque, which puts God's stamp of approval on the process. The stones are specially selected. They are relatively small, smaller than a tennis ball, for example, small enough so that no single stone can kill, or even come close to killing. And the stones are thrown by the people who happen to pass by. Each person throws one stone, then moves along. They don't stay around and gawk, and they can't decline to throw a stone. It's part of the process."

I stared at him in rapt fascination as he continued.

"You see, the purpose of stoning is only partly to kill the offender. It's also done to establish the killing of the offender as the collective judgment and punishment of *all* the people. When someone throws a stone, he is participating in the judgment that has been passed, and the sentence that has been meted out. By so participating, the seriousness of the offense and the inevitable nature of the punishment are indelibly engraved on the mind and heart of the greatest number of people."

The room was completely silent for several seconds.

Finally, I spoke. "That's a tough thing for us to imagine," I said, speaking for all my countrymen. I looked Mr. Nazer in the eye. "Do *you* have any problem with it?"

He shrugged his shoulders and smiled a barely perceptible smile. "Allah has spoken. Who am I to ask why?"

That statement effectively ended the discussion.

The meeting continued for quite a while, but the subject turned to the finer points of our client's situation and Mr. Nazer's suggestions as to how we should proceed. When our session ended, I barely had time to get him to his flight. After we parted, I neither saw him nor spoke to him again.

For days after he left, I thought a great deal about what he had said.

The idea of someone being pummeled to death, one small stone at a time, chilled me to the bone. I couldn't get the image out of my mind. What a slow, painful, agonizing way to die. And how must the people feel who *throw* those stones? Can they do something like that without being deeply involved emotionally? Perhaps it's so much a part of their culture that they are immune to its impact; perhaps they have come to regard it as routine.

I would like to have heard more from Mr. Nazer. I wish I had found out if he had ever thrown one of those stones. My impression was that he had, but he had closed the door on that subject without volunteering the information, and I had felt obliged to extend him the courtesy of not asking.

But what if he *had*? What if he had *told* me about it, so I could be sure? Would I have regarded him any differently? Would I have *treated* him any differently?

As the early church grew, administrative problems frequently developed. In one instance, there was a controversy concerning the way the wives of the Orthodox Jews from Palestine were treated, as compared with the treatment given the wives of the Orthodox Jews who were not native Palestinians, with regard to the distribution of the public stores. So the disciples found it necessary to come together and work the problem out.

Like any good church group, they formed a committee.

A young disciple named Stephen was chosen to head that committee, and apparently he did a pretty good job.

The chronicle of this venture, and how it fared, is found in the sixth and seventh chapters of Acts (NKJ).

Stephen was "full of faith and power," so we are told, and he "did great wonders and signs among the people" (6:8). But as luck would have it, not everyone liked him or approved of his solutions. A dispute arose, and because they weren't "able to resist the wisdom and the Spirit by which he spoke," his enemies bore false witness against him. Because they did so, he was arrested and taken before the council. There, his enemies swore that Stephen had claimed that Jesus would destroy the Temple and the Law of Moses.

Stephen's defense was stirring, emotional, and very forceful. He let the council know in no uncertain terms that he hadn't done *any* of the acts of which he stood accused. Nonetheless, the council accepted the testimony of the false witnesses, and Stephen was delivered into the hands of the people to suffer the wrath of their judgment.

Before I met Ismail Nazer, I was able to read the story of Stephen in the Bible with little more than dispassionate interest. But after hearing my Saudi colleague's story about the continuing practice of the ancient custom of stoning, I can understand more clearly the plight of the young disciple who was described as having "the face of an angel" (6:15).

I can see Stephen in my mind's eye, standing before the multitude, his countenance reflecting a spirit of acceptance, an inner peace, which no doubt served only to fan the fires of his enemies.

I can see the small stones flying at him one at a time. I can see him enduring their blows until they had bruised and battered him, finally crushing his flesh and allowing death to release his spirit.

I can see the faces of the people who threw the stones. Somehow I don't picture them as being determined and duty-bound, as described by my friend from Saudi

Arabia. I see them as being arrogantly self-righteous, quick to pass judgment on the strength of a pack of lies, individually venting their anger by the hurling of a stone, relishing the sound it made as it struck Stephen's flesh, relishing even more his anguished cries.

Seeing that spectacle in my mind's eye makes that story from the Book of the Acts of the Apostles even more remarkable.

> And they stoned Stephen as he was calling on God and saying, "Lord Jesus, receive my spirit."
> Then he knelt down and cried out with a loud voice, "Lord, do not charge them with this sin." And when he had said this, he fell asleep. (7:59-60 NKJ)

Remarkable, isn't it? That Stephen could forgive at a time like that? The grace that comes from God, the grace that filled Stephen's heart, the grace that flows through *us* when we forgive those who have sinned against us, truly is amazing.

There was another young man on hand that day as the people executed their sentence against Stephen. A man from Tarsus. A man named Saul.

The Bible doesn't tell us that Saul took his turn and threw a stone. Instead, he watched over the garments of the witnesses, consenting fully to this needless, unjust cruelty.

After that incident, Saul persecuted Christians throughout the land, "breathing threats and murder against the disciples of the Lord" (9:1).

When Jesus met Saul on the road to Damascus, Saul had no defense against the Savior's indictment. Yet it was Saul whom Jesus chose and Saul whom Jesus forgave.

Once Saul had accepted Jesus' gift of grace and repented of his sins, no single human being, apart from

Christ himself, did more to foster the growth of the Christian movement or to inspire future generations.

If God can give a man like Stephen the strength to endure the horrors of being stoned and the compassion to forgive his accusers, *surely* he can do the same for us.

If God can forgive the likes of Saul of Tarsus, a bitter, active enemy of the faith; if God's love and grace can enable such a wretch to become Saint Paul, *surely* God can forgive *us*.

With God's grace and his power in our hearts, perhaps *we* can find the compassion to forgive *our* enemies, too.

The Samaritan with Very Good Intentions

— · —

ONE AFTERNOON MANY YEARS AGO, my wife Barbara happened to be in a store that does custom framing and also features an impressive collection of original works of art. While she was there, she spent so much time admiring the art and became so engrossed in her surroundings, that time simply got away from her. Concerned about being late, she asked a friend who worked at the store if she could use the telephone. The friend led Barbara to an office in the back.

Once she was alone, Barbara picked up the phone, dialed a number, and waited. While she was waiting, she noticed a motto hanging on the wall behind her friend's desk.

It struck an immediate responsive chord.

Barbara jotted the motto down and gave it to me that evening:

> Character
> is seeing the task through
> *after* the mood is gone.

Some time after Barbara's experience with her friend's motto, she and I heard a sermon in our church based on the scriptural story of the good Samaritan. It was a good sermon with a good message, but it pretty much stuck with the standard approach to that story. It dealt with unselfishness, our responsibility to our neighbors, and our need to define more broadly our concept of just who our "neighbors" might be.

In the middle of that sermon, my mind wandered back to the motto Barbara had seen on that wall. But it didn't stop there. It kept on wandering, carrying me all the way back to my first year in high school, back to my freshman Latin class.

You see, that classroom also had a motto on the wall:

Honor, Truth, and Integrity;
these are the things that stand.

As I listened to the rest of that sermon, it occurred to me that the innkeeper in that story might well have had *both* mottoes on display in his establishment.

The story of the good Samaritan is one of the most familiar and most beautiful in all of biblical literature.

In chapter ten of the Gospel According to Luke, Jesus is approached by a lawyer with an attitude. This lawyer wants to test Jesus, so he asks him a question:

"Teacher, what shall I do to inherit eternal life?" (10:25)

Jesus responds with a question of his own:

"What is written in the law?" (10:26)

The lawyer answers without hesitation:

"You shall love the LORD your God with all your heart, with all your soul, with all your strength, and with all your mind, and your neighbor as yourself." (10:27)

Jesus confirms the correctness of the lawyer's response, but the lawyer isn't finished yet. He has one more question:

"And who is my neighbor?" (10:29b)

That's when Jesus relates the familiar tale of a traveler on the road from Jerusalem to Jericho. This traveler is otherwise unidentified. He could have been anyone.

While on the road, this traveler was accosted by thieves who beat him, robbed him, and left him by the side of the road, where he would surely die.

A priest happened by. So did a Levite. Both were repulsed by the sight of the man on the side of the road; both walked on by without offering aid.

Then along came a Samaritan. He cleaned the man's wounds with the medicines he had on hand, placed the man on his animal, took him to an inn, and took care of him overnight. The next morning, he gave the innkeeper some money to cover the man's care, and agreed to cover any additional expenses when he passed by again.

Like the unknown soldier, this nameless Samaritan carved a place of honor for himself on the tablets of history.

In that humble inn beside a dusty road, in the first glow of a new day, the innkeeper and the Samaritan struck a bargain. They agreed between themselves that the Samaritan could leave the injured man in the care of the innkeeper, who would do whatever he could to see the man back to health, and then send him on his way to complete his journey. The Samaritan would go back to his travels, but he would return. He would leave some money with the innkeeper and pay the balance on his next trip that way.

The mood in that inn must have been one of charity, kindness, and noble self-sacrifice. No doubt both of those men were caught up in the wonder of the moment, basking in the glow of a truly good deed. It may be that they shook hands or embraced to seal the bargain.

After that, the Samaritan probably had his morning meal, then left. Later that day, the innkeeper might well have slipped away from his duties long enough to look in on his patient. None of this is known for sure, because at that point, the scene shifts. Luke's pen carries us from the inn to a village called Bethany, to the home of a woman named Martha. In that setting, we learn about another incident. Another story is told, and another point is made.

But the story of the good Samaritan isn't really over at the time of the agreement. Yes, something very important happened at that inn. Two men made significant promises to each other, and then separated. Neither had the power to *make* the other perform. Each of the two had to depend on the other, and each knew that the other was depending on him.

Each *also* knew that no one would be watching.

The Samaritan chose to rely on the character of the innkeeper, believing that he would, indeed, follow through after the good mood of the moment was over, believing that he would care for the injured man and use the money only for that purpose. The innkeeper chose to rely on the integrity of the Samaritan, believing that he would, indeed, return and pay the rest of the bill. And in *both* cases, character and integrity were put to the test where most of life's difficult tests take place—deep inside each man's heart, away from the intrusive view of any other human being.

Sad to say, it probably wouldn't happen that way today. The story of the good Samaritan would probably have to be called "The Samaritan with Very Good Intentions."

Consider the realities of our modern world.

If anyone *did* pause to look sympathetically at a fallen traveler lying beside a dusty road, he or she probably would be too afraid of the consequences to get involved. He might have the *heart* of a good Samaritan, but his *brain* would be fully aware of the potential for liability.

But what if someone *did* stop to minister to the traveler and then carry him to a nearby inn? The story would fall completely apart the instant the modern-day Samaritan suggested to the innkeeper that he attend to the needs of the wounded traveler and foot the bills until the Samaritan happened by again.

For openers, the twentieth-century Samaritan would want a written contract with the innkeeper, and a trust agreement governing the disbursement of funds left on deposit for the traveler's care. He would dislike the idea of leaving cash, but he might agree to do that rather than reveal his credit-card number to a virtual stranger.

The innkeeper, offended by the Samaritan's desire for contractual protection, probably would protect himself and his business by demanding an escrow arrangement and a letter of credit, whereby additional funds would be guaranteed available should the Samaritan fail to return.

Both men would want to learn about the tax consequences resulting from the transfer of funds and extending of services. And how would these matters be entered on their books?

Both men would want a signed release from the traveler, protecting them from liability in the event that the traveler should fail to recover from his wounds, or should deteriorate further as a result of his grievous injuries, or should retain residual disability at the end of the healing process. The traveler would be in no condition to *sign* such a release, so the Samaritan and the innkeeper would have to jointly petition the local court for the appointment of a guardian to sign all appropriate documents on the traveler's behalf.

The Samaritan and the innkeeper would want releases from each other, too.

At this point, the lawyers, accountants, and bankers for each side would be called in and everything else would stop. No point in drawing up elaborate, expensive documents if the traveler's guardian won't sign them.

While this was going on, a guest at the inn would become concerned about the groans of the injured traveler. Acting anonymously to protect himself, he would notify the authorities that something strange was happening in the room down the hall. The police, having heard only one side of the story, would respond in full force, swooping down on the inn and hauling everyone off. Several days would be taken up by court appearances, but even when the red tape had been cut and the truth revealed, the authorities wouldn't let the innkeeper care for the traveler, because neither he nor the inn had ever registered as a properly licensed health-care provider.

The licensing process would consume even more time.

Eventually that barrier would be hurdled, only to be replaced by yet another. The innkeeper would have to remodel his inn to comply with OSHA regulations. He would have to build wheelchair ramps, enlarge his bathrooms, and install an elevator.

After *that* had been accomplished, the harried innkeeper would be required to choose a health plan and select a primary physician. The innkeeper and the primary physician would then submit a treatment plan to the traveler's insurance carrier (no pun intended), which would eventually decide how much care the traveler could receive. Meantime, the guardian would be appointed and would request an *independent* examination of the traveler, to be sure that the treatment suggested by the insurance carrier was the best possible choice.

More time would pass.

Once that matter was resolved, the lawyers, accountants, and bankers would re-enter the picture. The final papers would be drawn by the lawyers, discussed over drinks, redrawn, rediscussed over dinner (all at their clients' expense, of course) and generally debated *ad nauseam*, in a successful effort to increase their billable hours.

Finally, the papers would be ready. Unfortunately, by the time both parties had signed them, the traveler would be dead—not from his wounds, but from old age.

It is highly unlikely that the traveler would be the only one harmed by this process. The innkeeper probably would have to file for bankruptcy protection, since his legal fees and building improvements would have eaten all his assets. Meanwhile, the business at his inn would have dried up due to the publicity generated by the anonymous irate guest. The Samaritan would have lost his job as a traveling merchant because of unauthorized absences from work, and he too would be drowning in red ink due to his enormous legal fees.

The Samaritan's *animal*, tired of waiting for something to happen, would have wandered off long ago.

Within mere days after this sad affair had drawn to a conclusion, the innkeeper would sign to appear on *Geraldo* and tell his story, which would, he hoped, catapult him to international notoriety. The Samaritan would offer *his* story to *Oprah*. Before either version made it to the television screen, however, the two men would get injunctions against each other, each claiming exclusive rights to the story.

The lawyers for both sides eventually would be indicted and convicted of conspiracy to overbill a client. They would be sentenced to long prison terms, but actually would serve only a fraction of their time due to prison overcrowding and lax sentencing laws. The jurors who convicted them would be irate over the brevity of their time served, but would be powerless to do anything.

Once they were released, the lawyers would become radio talk-show hosts.

The heirs of Saint Luke would sue *both* the innkeeper *and* the Samaritan for copyright infringement.

Hard Copy and *A Current Affair* would get into a bidding war over the services of the whistle blower, the irate guest. In the end, the irate guest would go public and reveal not only his identity, but also the morbid details of the affair. He would end up doing this on *both* of those shows, *and* on *20/20*, becoming wealthy in the process.

He would tell a different version each time.

His avowed reason for appearing on those shows, of course, would have nothing whatever to do with money. It would be to keep this kind of thing from happening to anyone else. An anxious nation would lap up his every word. He would be flooded with job offers and marriage proposals. Newspapers and TV commentators would dub him "America's Favorite Irate Guest," and he would be virtually assured of a career in second-rate motion pictures.

That wouldn't happen until *after* the Barbara Walters and Larry King interviews, of course.

Much like the Samaritan's animal, honor, truth, and integrity would be lost in the shuffle. The "mood" of the moment would be selfishness, not satisfaction. What happens *after* the mood would be irrelevant, since the mood would never end.

Far-fetched? Maybe so, but painfully possible nonetheless. After all, don't *each* of those possibilities happen all the time these days?

During the weeks that followed my hearing of that sermon, I had lunch with two men, one at a time, on different days.

The first man was the head of the claims department at a large insurance company. He controlled a vast amount of legal business, and he was looking me over, to see if he wanted to put me on his list of attorneys.

During lunch, our conversation stayed on a light plane,

with him asking questions for the most part, and me providing answers. We lingered over coffee and continued to talk, but as our time together drew to a close, he seemed dissatisfied and restless.

I couldn't figure out what was wrong.

The dining room was almost empty. The noisy noontime crowd had come and gone. Except for our talk, the only sound was the clatter of dishes as the waiters and waitresses cleaned up from the meal.

My guest stopped asking questions and started to tell me about himself.

"I'm a committed Christian," he began.

During the next several minutes, he told me about his conversion experience and what it had meant to him. He told me how his professional life had changed as a result. He told me that it was his intention that the lawyers he worked with handle his cases in a manner consistent with timeless Christian principles.

As the head of an insurance company's claims department, this man had to make decisions regarding the disbursement or withholding of huge sums of money, usually in situations where the potential recipient was in great distress and serious need. His success would be measured in large part by the amount of money he saved his company in the process. I had seen instances where such motivation had led to abuse, unfairness, and inequality. But *this* man let me know that *his* commitment was to fairness, compassion, and caring.

I looked forward to working with him with great excitement.

The second lunch was equally interesting, but altogether different.

That man was the project manager for a multinational construction company. Like my first lunch guest, he was charming, likable company.

We had been together several days, working on a major case. We had reached the point when we needed to make contact with a potential witness, the head of another corporation. That other person had once been president of my lunch companion's construction company, but he had left the company under less-than-ideal circumstances. In the process he had made several enemies, including my lunch guest. Now, we needed him to testify. I was seriously concerned about his attitude. Would he help us? Would he be vindictive?

I asked my lunch guest for an evaluation of this man.

"I got a call from him last year," my lunch guest responded. "We hadn't talked to each other for a long time, and the call surprised me. I had experienced some serious health problems, and this man had heard about them. Fortunately, the problems had been resolved successfully."

"Was that all the call was about?" I asked.

"That's just how it *began*," he responded. "He told me that he was a new person. He had been 'born again,' and had joined a weekly prayer group. He wanted me to know that his prayer group had been praying for my recovery. I was skeptical, given our prior relationship, but I gave him the benefit of the doubt and thanked him. Then he moved on to the *real* purpose of his call."

"Which was . . ."

"A business opportunity, and a plan for our two companies to jointly take advantage of it. Our company would provide the money, and his company would handle the details. I listened, but it soon became apparent that this so-called opportunity was really nothing more than a chance to take unfair advantage of a person who was in trouble. The plan he proposed was devious, cunning, conniving, underhanded, unethical, and bordered on being illegal. Its only redeeming qualities were that it would be easy to accomplish, and very profitable."

"How did you handle it?"

"I managed to stay civil, but I declined firmly. And I got off the phone as quickly as I possibly could."

My lunch guest never asked me what I believed or where I stood. He simply told me that story. And he finished with these exact words, words I shall never forget:

"Richard, I'm not a Christian myself. I really don't know *what* I believe, but I know I'm not a Christian."

He leaned forward and pointed his finger at me to emphasize what he was about to say.

"I'll guaran-damn-tee you *one* thing, though. With Christians like *that* one out there running around, I'm *never* gonna be one."

If the story of the good Samaritan happened today, what role might these two men play—my first lunch guest and my second guest's friend?

Which one would have finished the task, in a Christian spirit, after the mood was gone? Which one would have demonstrated honor, truth, and integrity by his actions?

Which one would be able to enjoy at night the untroubled sleep of a peaceful heart?

Do It Yourself, If You Dare

— . —

I STILL REMEMBER THE DARK, DARK DAY I first decided to do-it-myself instead of paying someone who knew what he was doing.

I was in my mid-twenties at the time—a dangerous age, to say the least. In their mid-twenties, men think they can do *anything*.

We had just moved into our first house, and everywhere I looked, I saw something that needed to be done. Unfortunately, I *also* saw an opportunity to save money by doing it myself.

The project in question, the first one I ever took on, involved the removal of a grubby old porcelain sink. It was in the kitchen, but it looked more like a laundry basin than anything else. It was wide, deep, stained, and scratched. The decision was easy. It *had* to go.

I marched out to the store and bought a new one—a double sink made of shiny stainless steel, complete with a single-handle faucet and a garbage disposal.

"Would you like to have it installed?" the clerk asked.

"No, I'll do it myself," I announced confidently.

"Would you like for me to get someone to carry it to your car?"

His insulting question triggered my manly instincts.

"I can handle it," I assured him.

One very sore back later, the stainless-steel sink and all

of its accompanying parts were sitting in the middle of our kitchen floor.

I rolled up my sleeves and dove right in. When I had finished, everything worked perfectly. There were no leaks, no problems, no unused pieces, and no leftover mess.

So why is this such a dark day in my memory?

There are times when success can be your enemy. At this point in my life, I'd give *anything* if that first project had been a failure. As it was, there was no turning back.

It was during the early stages of that project that I first learned Rule Number One for all do-it-yourselfers. It is this: You begin by tearing down, not by building up.

Here's why.

Home-improvement projects never exist separate and apart from the home itself, or from the family living there, and there is *never* unanimity over whether the project is needed, or wanted. In fact, most of the time, it's us against them. *All* of them. So the first thing you do in any project is to grab your tools and utterly destroy the old before anyone has a chance to stop you, explaining as you go that such a move on your part was necessary.

Faced with the prospect of living in a partially wrecked house, most members of your family will rally to your side, or at the very least, resign themselves to the inevitable.

Clever, huh?

Following that principle to the max, I had made certain that the old sink I was removing broke into pieces the minute I started pushing on it. I thereby eliminated all my wife's arguments against my taking on such a difficult task. At the same time, however, it afforded her a splendid opportunity to let me know how upset she was about the incredible mess I was creating.

So, it's a trade-off. Only *you* can decide which you'd rather hear—pleading or complaining.

Down through the years, I have applied that "mess it up before fixing it up" principle to a number of projects.

I wanted to build a patio, so I dug up four hundred square feet of lush grass, roots and all. Never mind the fact that I ended up with a nondescript concrete slab in my backyard, one that looked like a heliport and was hopelessly bereft of grace and charm.

I needed to install a humidifier on our heater, so I punched through the main air-outflow duct with my trusty sabre saw and cut out a hole which, by pure coincidence, turned out to be just the right size for the desired appliance. I was a bit nervous for a while about that one, what with all that expensively heated air pouring out into the previously unheated basement, but I eventually got the thing installed.

Not all my projects were as modestly successful as those two, especially during the in-progress stage. Take, for example, the time I put in a new hot-water heater.

With the water heater, I more or less skipped Rule One. The old one had quit heating water to an acceptable temperature. I didn't have to convince anyone that we needed a new one. On the other hand, I *did* have to cut some copper water pipes, and that's when things began to unravel right before my helpless eyes.

Let me set the stage.

The water heater I needed to replace was in our attic, accessible only by a very steep, very narrow set of pull-down stairs. That was okay, though. I wasn't going to *live* up there, just do a little work.

The first problem I faced was how to get the new water heater up the stairs. It was quite bulky and remarkably heavy, even without any water in it. The stairs were too narrow for me to stand to one side and haul the cumbersome appliance while holding it next to me, and when I tried climbing *up* first, there wasn't any way to get

73

enough leverage to pull it up after me. The only choice was to squat down, wiggle my way *under* the heater, and push it up the stairs by brute force.

I quickly learned that *this* brute doesn't have all that much force.

I maneuvered myself under the water heater by the hardest, and I even managed to stand upright with its weight on my shoulders. But what was I to do next? Logic dictated that I raise one foot and place it on the first step, and then repeat that process until I had scaled them all. But the water heater was so heavy that I feared that neither of my legs, acting alone, would be able to hold the weight by itself. In my mind's eye, I could see my leg buckling. I even worried that if I *were* successful in climbing the wooden stairs, one of the steps might splinter under the load. I was totally ignorant as to their weight-bearing capacity.

Frankly, these are the kinds of problems that ought to be identified and solved *before* the project is undertaken, not afterward.

Anyway, there I was, immobilized in mid-hoist, totally at a loss as to what to do next.

To the best of my memory, what I *did* was to scream at the top of my lungs until someone would hear me and come running. Unfortunately, no one heard me, so I quit screaming, summoned my courage, and took the first step.

In minutes, the water heater was in the attic, and my troubles were over.

Well, as it turned out, my troubles were only *half* over.

When I cut the copper pipe that came out of the bottom of the unit, hot water started spraying all over me! What did I do? I panicked, of course, and stuffed my finger into the pipe. My finger wasn't quite the right shape, however, so instead of *stopping* the flow, all I accomplished was to cause several streams of very hot water to spray out at odd angles.

My finger felt as if it were cooking!

I screamed again.

My wife heard me this time and came running. When she saw me, she burst into laughter! I hastily let her know that I needed *help*, not laughter. I needed something to catch the hot water.

Responding like a pro, she grabbed the baby's plastic bathtub and tossed it up to me. I spent the rest of the afternoon filling the baby's bathtub full of hot water and handing it down the folding stairs, which was no easy task, when you consider that I had to do it with one hand while the other continued to partially plug the pipe.

You would think that the memory of such an experience would last a lifetime, but not so. Several years later I found myself in a very similar predicament when I tried to install a sixteen-foot-wide solid-steel garage door.

According to the instructions, I was supposed to fasten the tracks into their proper places in the garage, prop the door upright in its closed position, install the lever arms, and then *lift* the door upward to the *open* position.

Once again I somehow managed to get my body under the weight, but believe me, this door was *much* heavier than the hot-water heater. I pressed upward with all my strength, forcing my legs to straighten. Finally, after a gargantuan effort, I was standing upright with several hundred pounds of steel resting on my shoulders.

What then? I stood there until someone came looking for me.

Those experiences were *bad*, but not bad enough to keep me from trying again. After all, how difficult could it be to install a ceiling fan?

I waited until my wife had gone away for the weekend so I could surprise her. She had always wanted a ceiling fan.

I began by crawling across the attic rafters to find the right spot. Once I was there, I cut a small hole in the porch ceiling, installed a junction box and bracket, then retraced my path. But on the way *back* across the rafters, I didn't crawl. I walked.

Big mistake. *Huge* mistake.

Near the end of my perilous journey, my foot slipped off one of the rafters. Down I went, *straight* down. My leg punched a hole in our living room ceiling, directly above our brand-new dark blue velvet sofa! I didn't break any bones, but I sent paint flecks, drywall pieces, and a fine, powdery plaster falling like rain all over the sofa!

The rest of my weekend was spent trying to clean up the mess.

After the initial shock had subsided, my wife and I were surprised to learn how many of our friends could relate similar experiences. *One* friend's story was even worse than *mine*.

I won't use his name. He'd *kill* me.

My friend's daughter had been in a serious accident and was recuperating at home. She was confined to bed and immobilized by a body cast. My well-meaning friend decided to put a ceiling fan in her room to make her more comfortable.

On *his* first trip across the attic he was tight-roping along a rafter when *both* feet slipped, causing *both* legs to explode through the ceiling right above his daughter's bed! Fortunately, he didn't land on top of her. *Un*fortunately, he landed with considerable force, straddling the rafter, and there he remained, kicking and screaming in indescribable pain, while his totally helpless, completely immobilized, drywall-covered daughter stared upward in panic-stricken disbelief.

What a warm, wonderful family moment *that* must have been.

I'm older and wiser now. These days, I'm much more willing to admit my ignorance and get the help I need. It's definitely available—many good books deal with every conceivable do-it-yourself situation. Most contain detailed, step-by-step instructions, and also feature illustrations to show what the finished project will look like if the job is done correctly.

Clear instructions and helpful illustrations. Armed with *that* kind of help, I'm much more likely to succeed.

That's a good principle to follow in all walks of life, isn't it—even in the very personal matter of faith in God. This is especially true for Christians.

Our faith, in its daily application to our lives, is a do-it-yourself project.

Make no mistake. God created heaven and earth, and all that dwells therein. Christ came to earth to show us a better way. God started the project for us, and Jesus took on the most difficult task himself. He paid the ultimate price, but he didn't *finish* the job.

He left that up to us.

Jesus taught us that if we are willing to accept him as our Savior, the old can be torn out of our lives and replaced with something new. The crooked can be made straight. The sinner can be made whole. But the finished product isn't delivered in its final form. Each of us has to accept Christ's precious gift, and then do our own part.

Help is available for leading the life of a believer.

When Jesus ascended into heaven, he had lived his life on earth in such a way as to provide a perfect illustration of the kind of life *we* need to live.

We *can* find peace on earth, the peace that passes all understanding, both within ourselves and with our fellow human beings.

We *can* find eternal peace when this life on earth is over. Jesus left us much more than just an illustration, as good as that was. He also left us a complete set of instructions.

It's called the Bible.

"Follow me," Jesus told us. "Put me first. Forsake all else. *Believe* in me. Do unto others. Feed my sheep."

It's right there in the Bible, everything we need. If we read it and actually let it become a part of our lives, we cannot fail. I know that's true because the Bible says it's so. I know that's true because I have *experienced* it for myself.

For Christians, the bottom line is this: If life isn't what we *want* it to be, it isn't the fault of the church, our religion, our faith, our Savior, or our God. We have no one to blame but ourselves.

We are the ones who must affirmatively accept the gift of grace that Jesus extended freely from the cross.

We are the ones who must feed his sheep.

We are the ones who *must* practice forgiveness in our own lives.

We are the ones he was talking to when he said, "Go ye into all the world, preaching the gospel to all creation."

Christianity, you see, is a do-it-yourself religion. It's *not* just a matter of believing, praying, and hoping something will happen. We are called to a life of action, example, evangelism, witnessing, and work.

Jesus left us the model, his life, and the manual, the Bible. It's up to *us* to do it ourselves.

Dear Lucy

■ ▪ ■

"W<small>HY DON'T YOU WRITE THIS YOURSELF?</small>" I asked her.

"I can't," she replied.

"Of course you can. You *lived* it."

"I get choked up just *talking* about it. I don't think I could *stand* to write about it. But I want this story told."

"Why?"

She paused and thought about my question.

"It's really for me. And for her. I want to remember what it felt like when I saw her that first time. I want *her* to remember, too."

It didn't take me long to decide.

"Okay," I said. "You tell it. I'll write it down."

She leaned back in her chair and closed her eyes. A calmness settled into her features. Then she began to speak:

— ▪ — ▪

It's *cold* in this motel room. Cold physically, and cold emotionally. Why did we choose such a sterile place to meet? There's no *life* here. Everything about this place is so plastic, so plain. This isn't a plain day. It's a *special* day.

I sit on the bed. I pace the floor. I sit back down. I don't know what to do with myself. I could try waiting patiently, of course, but that's out of the question. I'm far too excited.

I'm also scared enough to be sick.

Dear God, don't let that happen. Not now. Not today.

I didn't get to see Lucy when she was born. The

efficient, antiseptic, unemotional staff at the hospital did what they had been told to do. They whisked her away while I drifted in and out of twilight sleep, leaving me with no chance to bond, no chance to change my mind.

I wasn't thinking about much of anything at that time, thanks to the drugs I had been given. I was *aware*, but I wasn't able to *care*. I *did* feel her leaving my body, though; I remember that quite clearly. But I didn't fully realize the impact of what I was experiencing. I didn't fully realize that she was also leaving my life.

In my heart I knew I would see her someday, even then.

All that happened more than twenty years ago.

Did I really make the decision to give her up? Was I old enough to make such a final, heart-wrenching decision? Or was I simply told that this was the way it was going to be? This was, after all, the way it was done back then. Teenage girls carried their shame to some remote place and came back nine months later empty-handed, ready to pick up where they had left off, ready to pretend that nothing had happened. Everyone around them—everyone around *me*—did the same thing. We pretended that nothing had happened. My heart had been crushed, but nothing was said.

What did I expect, that they would welcome their unmarried daughter's baby with open arms? They carried their own emotional baggage, just as I did. *I* acted, they *reacted*. This was as new for them as it was for me.

In the end, it became the family secret.

No, I couldn't blame it on someone else. That would've been too easy, too convenient. *I* did it. I let myself get pregnant, and I was willing to do whatever I had to do to get my life back in order. Even give her up.

Yes, the responsibility is mine. So is the pain.

It took me far longer to understand that than it took me to find Lucy, once I had summoned the courage to look.

Lucy. I never saw her, but she was always mine. My body protected her; my heart went with her when she left.

Each child has a special place in its mother's heart. I know that now. When that place is empty, the pain never goes away. It gnaws at you like a dull ache, always present, sometimes repressed, never completely forgotten. Sometimes, when least expected, that pain suddenly occupies center stage, demanding attention, requiring action.

That's what finally happened.

But why? Why after all these years?

To find the answer, I had to look at a bigger picture.

All of the areas of my life are suffering through an intense examination. My marriage, my relationship with my two daughters—my *other* two daughters—my self-respect, all are being dragged into the naked light of day.

My two little girls, both toddlers, are the jewels of my life. I could not possibly love them any more than I do. But they haven't *filled* that gap, only exposed it for what it is. They teach me every day that life is precious and that it should be affirmed. *All* life. Mine, theirs, even *hers*, the daughter I have never seen.

Once I decided, I knew my mother could help. Even though we've never said a word to each other about it, I knew. On the next trip home I swallowed my resentment, gathered my strength, and told her about the longing in my soul. Her reaction surprised me. Is it possible that the years have changed *her*, too? Is my heart not the only one carrying scars from that experience?

"Of course I'll help," she said, and then she hugged me.

We talked, woman to woman, about the pain I never thought we would be able to share. She cared as much as I did, as it turned out, and for once we were able to move toward the same goal, hand in hand.

What a shame. Each of us had been caught up in our

own feelings for so long that neither of us had ever realized how much the other had suffered.

Lucy was the name she had been given. Maybe that's what she was still called. And mother also knew the name of the family I had stayed with when I'd been sent away in secrecy, a "nice" girl gone wrong.

That family remembered me. They also remembered Lucy. Yes, that name had survived intact. They even knew the family with whom she had been placed.

I was excited to be learning so much, so fast, but the trail quickly ran out. When Lucy was eight, they had left the area, headed for another state, and soon had been lost in the anonymity of life.

Suddenly my pain was that much greater. Eight years! She had been *right there* for eight years! Why hadn't I tried earlier? Was I too late? It was no use. I had a name, but nothing else. Every road led to a cliff; every idea produced only frustration.

I even thought about quitting. Who needs this?

I need this, *that's* who.

Back to the telephone.

It became a part of our routine. The girls played or did their work, my husband read a book or watched TV, and I made telephone calls to total strangers, not all of whom liked what I was doing.

There's more than one side to this. I know that. My pain may end, but others may just be beginning to hurt. I hate that. I don't want to mess up anybody's life. I just want to *know*, that's all. I just want to patch up this hole in my heart as best I can.

Timing is important. So is luck. So is perseverance. Which one was it? I don't know. All I know is that after what seemed like forever, one of the calls finally paid off.

"Sure, I know that family," the helpful voice said. "Hang on a minute. I'll get you the number."

I held the slip of paper in my hand and stared at it. Oh my God, I thought. I've run out of excuses.

I turned to my husband. *"You'll* have to make this call." He was glad to help.

I listened while he dialed the number. I was petrified with fear, scared they wouldn't answer, even *more* scared that they *would!*

Someone answered. It was a woman—Lucy's adoptive mother.

My husband explained who he was, and who *I* was. She didn't hang up on him. I thanked God for that, but I also felt this incredible wave of guilt. How would *she* feel, this woman who has loved my child all these years? How much would *she* suffer over this?

I almost told him to hang up. Almost. But I couldn't do it. The longing was too great. I *had* to go forward.

"She gave me an address," he said when the conversation was over. "She thinks you ought to write her, not call her. She says you need to go slow."

We hugged. We cried. We hugged some more, and we cried some more. Then I stared at the address, but it didn't matter where she was. I'd go *anywhere.*

But I *couldn't* go slow.

I called information. There was no phone number listed in her name. I called that town's public library. The reference room identified the address as an apartment complex. After a few more calls, I had the apartment manager on the line. He was willing to leave a note on her door; *she* would have to decide whether to call.

"Please hurry," I begged him.

He said he would.

"Tell her she can call collect, any time, day or night," I pleaded. "Tell her we're going to wait right here until she calls."

I hung up.

"She'll think we're crazy," I told my husband. "She'll never call. I just *know* it."

He took me in his arms. "You've done all you can," he assured me.

I knew he was right. I couldn't *make* it happen, I could only pray that it would.

Three hours later, it did.

My husband answered the phone. I listened from an extension. It should have been *me* doing the talking, but I couldn't. I was too scared. I couldn't *move,* much less speak. My heart was filled with emotions so wild and varied that I couldn't identify them, let alone *control* them.

"Is this some kind of a joke?" she asked. I was crushed. But what did I expect? It's been twenty-two years!

My disappointment quickly faded. I kept reminding myself that he was actually talking to my daughter! I did that over and over again in my mind, as if *repeating* it might help me to *believe* it.

The conversation ended.

"It's going to be all right," he assured me. Then he reminded me of what she had said. Yes, she would see me, but first she wanted a letter, and some pictures.

That very night, I sat down to write. I didn't know what to say, but I *did* know how to *start.*

Dear Lucy, I wrote.

— · — · —

When was the last time I watched for the mailman every day? Never, that I could recall. I felt like a teenager with a crush on someone, but that's not what I was. I was a woman, trying to build a bridge twenty-two years long.

And wouldn't you know I wouldn't be there when it arrived!

My husband was holding the letter when I walked through the door. His smile said it all. I screamed with delight and tore open the envelope.

I stared dumbly at the picture.

She's a *woman*, I thought. What happened to her childhood? Where are all those years? All those unshared memories? What have I *missed*?

Sadness filled my heart, but I didn't let it stay. Instead, my mind raced ahead to the good things yet to come. This is no time to live in the past. *This* is a time to *rejoice*!

Lucy picked the place. She wasn't ready to take me home yet, and I didn't blame her. I wasn't ready for that either. She picked the place, and we agreed on a time. When the day arrived, we checked in as early as possible. Then my husband called her.

"We're here," is all he said.

_. _. _

I pace, I sit, I pace some more. I wait for a knock on the door. I wait for my oldest daughter. My little girl.

Is this really happening? Twenty-two years, and she's finally on her way. What will she look like in person? My God, what will *I* look like to *her*? Will she like me? Am I wearing the right thing? It's not too late to change . . .

What *difference* does it make? This is my *child*, my *flesh*, my *heart*, my *soul*. Nothing else matters.

I know that's true, but it doesn't keep my mind from racing, my stomach from churning, or my knees from knocking.

I hear a sound. It's very light, so light that I almost miss it. It comes again.

It's the door.

My husband glances my way. I rise slowly, step forward, and face the door as he opens it.

My heart races. Words escape me. I am overwhelmed, suspended in disbelief.

"Well hello," Lucy says awkwardly. Then she smiles. "I'm *here!*"

Forty Jewels from a Church-Camp Wall

— . —

Each summer, countless happy, healthy young people leave their homes and head for church camp, knowing they will return with arms and legs covered with chigger bites and hearts filled with good memories. At the same time, thousands of nervous, apprehensive church-camp counselors head in the same direction, hoping to be able to return with their sanity intact.

Church camp was a big deal when I was growing up. Year after year, church camp was one of the highlights of my summer.

I went every summer from the age of eight on, usually for a week at a time. There, in the company of other budding Christians, I explored the wonders of a relationship with God, and flirted with the devil as much as I could without getting caught. The impact on my spiritual life was always significant, although I must admit that as I entered my teenage years, the exploring/flirting ratio tipped decidedly in the devil's direction.

The same group of young people from my church went every year. Our camp was located, appropriately enough, on top of a mountain. It was rustic, to be sure, but adequate for our needs.

The centerpiece of the camp was an old hotel, a gorgeous multifloored white frame building with expansive balconies and incredibly dilapidated rooms. Then again, what rooms *wouldn't* be dilapidated after being occupied all summer by an ever-changing gang of hyperactive thyroids, intent on destroying everything in sight.

I stayed in one of those dismal hotel rooms during my first visit to that camp, and I learned a valuable lesson in the process. Every year thereafter, I made it a point to arrive early enough to claim one of the cabins. I would have come *days* early if necessary. Those rooms were *grim*.

The hotel had a huge main room filled with various kinds of game tables. There was also a spacious dining room. The setting was spartan, but the food was good and there was always plenty of it. The thing I remember most about the dining room is not the food, however, but the singing. We sang camp songs after every meal. Somehow, they always managed to find us a song leader who knew how to strip us of our inhibitions, and who did so on the very first day. Two hundred enthusiastic teenagers singing at the top of their lungs could shake the rusty nails right out of those old wooden rafters!

From the hotel's spacious balconies, and from the stone patio across the road from the hotel's entrance, the view was simply breathtaking. Lush valleys stretched endlessly in every direction.

The view was equally impressive and inspiring from the outdoor chapel down the road from the hotel, where we had vespers every evening.

When I stopped going to church camp, I had no idea I would never again enjoy the blessing of daily vespers.

Just before sunset, my friends and I would gather, wander down the road to the chapel, and claim a space on the splintery wooden benches that had been arranged in a semicircle several centuries earlier. Of course I'm estimating the age of those benches based on their condition; I really don't know how long they had been there.

Every seat faced the cross, a full-size, rough-edged replica hewn from local timber. Beyond the cross lay the peaceful, welcoming valley.

Looking back, I realize that the setting was something of a metaphor for our faith.

The seating arrangement at vespers was a matter of critical importance. My friends and I always jockeyed for position, scrambling to find a place next to that "special someone," which posed a problem when more than one person thought the same "someone" was special. Eventually, though, we all managed to find a seat. After that, we were reasonably still and relatively quiet. The setting didn't lend itself to much horseplay.

Mealtime *ended* with singing. Vespers *began* that way.

There's something really special about church-camp songs. They have a simplicity about them, a clarity which makes their purpose unmistakable and their effect unavoidable. When we climbed Jacob's ladder, we ascended emotionally, step by step. We really *felt* that joy, joy, joy, joy down in our hearts. For a few precious moments, we were one in the Spirit, one in the Lord.

If we can't bring back vespers, perhaps we can sing some of those wonderful camp songs in our churches every now and then.

I've been told that more young people make the decision to commit themselves to full-time Christian work at church camps than in any other setting. I expect that's true, and I'll bet it happens more often at vespers than at any other time, while everyone is sitting next to that special someone, holding hands, joining voices in song.

Of course not everyone makes a permanent commitment to God, not even in *that* setting, but for most attendees, church camp is a place where faith can be shared openly with people of the same age, without fear of being put down in any way.

During my teenage years, I had a very close friend who was a member of another denomination. His church camp experience took place atop a different mountain.

Are *all* church camps located on top of mountains? Maybe it just *seems* that way, because of the mountain-top experiences they almost always provide.

Anyway, my friend went to camp most summers, just as I did. *I* always came home with pleasant memories, sleep-deprived eyes, a backache from lying on a lumpy mattress, and a world-class collection of chiggers. *He* invariably came home with a broad smile on his face and vivid memories of some gorgeous young thing who had fallen madly in love with him in the space of one short week. He shared those memories freely.

For a long time I suspected that my friend was making those stories up to get my goat, but one year I actually got to meet his latest summer romance. She was every bit as pretty as he had described her, and every bit as taken with him, too.

When I went away to college, I became a church-camp dropout. As wonderful as the experience had been *every single time*, decades would pass before I found myself in that kind of rustic, serene setting again.

The occasion was a Men's Weekend Retreat.

We didn't have vespers that weekend, but we had services at the outdoor chapel overlooking the lake. The setting was as beautiful and inspiring as any I remembered from my youth. Just being in that spot, seeing the old rugged cross set against a background of tranquil water and lush green forest, brought back some truly wonderful memories.

Some time during that weekend, during one of our free periods, I wandered over to the great hall and read all the words of wisdom that had been pinned on the walls.

The great hall was the room where campers of all ages

traditionally gathered for their meals and for fellowship together. Earlier, while standing in line at mealtime, I had noticed all those little white cards on the walls, and I wanted to take another look.

Clearly, young people had written many of those messages. There was a freshness about the way the thoughts were expressed, to say nothing of the youthful handwriting. Some were serious, some were light-hearted, but all were meaningful, relevant, and universal in their appeal.

How did this get started? I have no idea. I could have asked, but I didn't bother. The truth might have spoiled things. I prefer to imagine that at some point in time, some searching soul was moved by God to jot down a favorite thought and put it up for others to read, as a sort of silent, continuing witness. Someone else discovered that first jewel of wisdom and was moved to follow suit. Then another did the same, and before long a tradition had been established.

By the time I arrived on the scene, those little handwritten cards and slips of paper covered an expansive chunk of wall.

I picked out my favorites, forty in number, and offer them to you.

Pass them on. They are worth sharing.

—·—·—

The race is always won by those who finish.

—·—·—

You can't steal second with your foot on first.

—·—·—

Faith isn't faith until it's all you have left to hold on to.

—·—·—

It's better to change your mind and succeed than to stand your ground and fail.

—·—·—

If you lose your *money* you have lost a little; if you lose
your *health* you have lost a lot;
if you lose your *courage* you have lost *everything*.

— · — · —

Life is a symphony.
How good it is depends on how it is conducted.

— · — · —

To see the creation is to know the creator.

— · — · —

Frustration is knowing exactly what you are supposed
to do, but not doing it.

— · — · —

Maturity is knowing the perfect put-down, but keeping
your mouth shut.

— · — · —

Touch the earth softly. Take only pictures,
leave only footprints.

— · — · —

Never turn a problem into an excuse.

— · — · —

It's not what *happens* to you that matters;
it's what you *become* as a result.

— · — · —

Thinking is the hardest work there is,
which explains why so few people do it.

— · — · —

The will to win is only as strong as the incentive to prepare.

— · — · —

The only person in the world you must be better than
is the person you are right now.

— · — · —

The future belongs to those who believe
in the beauty of their dreams.

— · — · —

Never let *anyone* dim your lights.

It only takes one negative person to kill your dream.

—.—.—

If the dream is big enough, the facts won't keep
it from coming true.

—.—.—

To keep someone from getting your goat,
don't tell them where it's tied.

—.—.—

It's better to be *happy* than *right*.

—.—.—

No one is a complete failure as long as he or she can
be used as a bad example.

—.—.—

There's no such thing as a bad day.
There are only good days and character-building days.

—.—.—

Wise people make commitments while foolish people
are making promises.

—.—.—

Never give an excuse you wouldn't be willing to accept
from someone else.

—.—.—

If you don't know what you are fighting for, why fight?

—.—.—

The trouble with self-made people is that they always
worship their creator.

—.—.—

Of all the things you wear, your facial expression is
by far the most important.

—.—.—

Never make a promise you know you can't keep.

—.—.—

Never make a promise you don't *intend* to keep.

—.—.—

Control is an illusion.

You may be disappointed if you fail, but you will be
doomed if you never try.

—·—·—

Most of us will never do great things.
All of us can do small things in a great way.

—·—·—

Never worry about what you have lost.
What's *important* is what you have *left.*

—·—·—

Pain and suffering are inevitable, but misery is optional.

—·—·—

The only person you can change is yourself.

—·—·—

The only person who can make you happy is the one
you see in the mirror.

—·—·—

Nobody notices what you do until you don't do it.

—·—·—

Don't let life's little problems get you down; that's what
the *big* problems are for.

—·—·—

If you put God first, you'll never come in second.

Bob, the Bearded Prophet

— · —

Bob WAS AN EASY MAN TO LIKE. He had a ruddy, smiling face that reflected his own contentment, sparkling eyes that revealed his emotions, and an easy disposition that made it possible for others to be comfortable in his presence.

He also had a salt-and-pepper beard which gave him the look of a biblical prophet. In fact, he often *played* such a biblical character in pageants and programs at our church. The wisdom, patience, and judgment he displayed in his real life were worthy of his role.

Bob had his bad times as well as his good, as we all do, but his inner core remained the same. That's what I admired most about him. When my life changed dramatically, his friendship and his attitude toward me remained the same. When our church changed dramatically, his presence and his participation remained steadfast. He was, in a word, dependable.

That's the word—dependable. There are people who have achieved such an inner satisfaction with themselves that they don't find it necessary to change when their circumstances change. Bob was one of those people.

Bob and I attended Sunday school together and served on many of the same boards and committees. I was brash, outspoken, and given to strong opinions. He was steady, patient, and temperate. We didn't always agree, but it never became personal. It was never me against him. In fact, we complemented each other rather nicely.

I was genuinely sad when I learned that Bob had died. I knew he had cancer, but like many others, I had been lulled into a false sense of security by his attitude. He never stopped smiling, and he never lost hope. He was the same old Bob, up until the end.

His memorial service drew a full house. That was no surprise. Family, friends, and acquaintances were present in abundance, sharing a common loss, leaning on one another.

I was the last person to arrive at the church. I settled into a folding chair against the back wall of the sanctuary. I couldn't see much, but I could hear, and I could reflect on what I heard.

Three ministers spoke that day.

The first was our minister emeritus. He spoke straight from the heart. He had known Bob well, so his words had the ring of truth as well as eloquence.

When he finished, there wasn't a dry eye in the place.

The second was a former minister of our church who had known great sorrow himself and had lost his own wife to cancer. He also spoke from the heart. He had remained close to Bob after leaving our church. They were the best of friends.

When *he* finished, you could have heard a pin drop.

The third speaker was an energetic young man whose ties to the deceased were fresh and relatively untested. He had just taken over the reins at our church, and there was little he could say of a personal nature. I felt a little sorry for him, having to follow two remarkably moving, intimate presentations.

My sympathy was unnecessary. He had the situation well in hand. He just let Bob speak for himself.

A few years earlier, while our church was between pastors, Bob had accepted the task of presenting a devotional at the monthly meeting of the church's governing board. His words on that particular evening had made quite an impression. When Bob died, someone in his family gave the new minister a copy of that final message from this gentle man.

As I listened, I was deeply moved.

After the memorial service had ended, I contacted Bob's family. They gladly gave me permission to share Bob's words in this book. The only change I have made is to delete specific references to our church and to its ministers. Bob's devotional could have been about almost anyone, and the church he refers to could be almost any church.

Bitterness was rampant in our church at the time Bob wrote these words. The congregation was sharply divided over issues that seemed important. Long-time members were leaving. Others were wavering. Still others were staying, but were being self-righteous and arrogant about it. Patience had been exhausted. Tolerance was in short supply. A voice of reason was sorely needed.

As always, God sent just the right voice at just the right time.

This is what Bob wrote:

It seems to me that most of what we hear, and read, and see today is based on the negative—the bad or sad things that happen to people, things like death, hunger, abuse, divorce—the list is endless. The world is in a sad state. Here at home the prisons are overflowing, the number of homeless is growing, money is tight, and people are out of work. Even here at our church, we have what seems to be an inordinate amount of trouble—sickness, divorce, death, job loss—and unhappy people. Yes, we even have disagreements within the church, and—I think it's okay to mention it—money problems. We're in turmoil. We wonder if it will ever be "wonderful" again.

97

Well, let me tell you my point of view.

It's my belief that I should only talk about those things that I know from first-hand knowledge. The best sermons I have ever heard were those that were the most personal. So, this is personal. These thoughts and feelings are mine, and they are real, because I was there.

At this church, I've had the very great pleasure, for one reason or another, of being pretty close to all of its ministers at every level of service, from the founding minister to the present. I've had occasion both to laugh and to cry with each one of them. I've loved them all, but on occasion I have been put out with each of them. You should understand, though, that the "love" part always survived. I believe our church is a better place because of each of them, but I *know* I am a better man.

Now, just for a moment, let me get very personal.

Some of you have known me for a long while, and some have not. I had a very happy marriage for thirty-seven years, and four better-than-average children who seem to improve with either their age or mine—I'm not quite sure which. Oh, we had our troubles—lack of money, sickness, loss of parents, problems raising children, general disagreements—the usual real-life problems everybody has, the kind you are certain no one else has ever experienced quite like you. But all in all, I had a very good marriage and a good life.

Then Lil, my wife, died. She had been sick for a very long time, and she died. That was the end. It was all over, and I knew it. No more *anything*—I couldn't live, eat, sleep, work—but I *had* to do those things.

It couldn't get worse, but it did.

After more than forty years with one company, doing a job and being in a business I thoroughly enjoyed, it became pretty obvious it wasn't going to last. Now what,

I wondered. Do I end up looking for a job at the age of sixty-one, on top of everything else? What a mess.

Was I depressed, unhappy, altogether miserable? *Of course!* Did I show it? Did I seek help? *Of course not!* Think about where people my age are coming from. *Real men plug on!*

I guess I did show it more than I thought, although as a rule, I wasn't very demonstrative or open. One Sunday at church, a perfectly lovely married lady asked me how I was doing.

"Just fine," says I.

"Well, you look to me like you need a hug," she responded.

So much for the "real man" idea. I got hugged, and I cried. That's love in *real* life. It works.

Somewhere, going through all of this, it occurred to me that I had really lost control.

You see, I always thought I had control of my life, my family, everything that concerned me. Not true. It slowly began to sink into this thick skull that I've had some choices and options, but I certainly didn't have control. I finally began to understand that control was in someone else's hands and that all I could do was to let him know, through prayer, what my hopes and fears were, and ask for strength and wisdom. I needed to quit fighting *myself.* I had to open my mind and my heart to who I was and where I was.

I hope this makes some sense to you; it does to me.

So, where am I now? I'm a very lucky man.

Lucky is really not the right word.

I have a new career in a growing company, resulting from an unsolicited offer. I'm having fun and enjoying myself at work more than I have in years.

More important, I became reacquainted with a perfectly delightful lady that I knew only slightly in high school and college. Very simply, Jane and I fell in love.

Unbelievable! We have been married for a little over seven very good months.

How could any man expect to be so blessed as to have a chance to love and be loved by not one, but *two* wonderful ladies in one short life? Well, it sure wasn't my *control* that did it. I leave you to figure it out for yourself.

Where in the world is all this going?

Let's see. I started out by talking about all the sad and bad things that have happened. We all know about, and personally experience, an almost overwhelming amount of sadness every day. Hopefully, we do our part to make things better as best we can.

But how about our blessings? Do we stop to consider *them*? Do we give thanks? Do we understand that the *real* control is not in us? In our private, public, and church life, is it possible that in our zeal, we are trying to impose our will on people and events, when we should be searching for *God's* will? Are we allowing the bad things to dominate? Are we trying to impose our agenda on others?

Let us not forget the *one thing* that survives all trials and tribulations. I'm speaking from personal experience. That one thing is love. The love of a wife (for me that's times two), the love of children (four plus three in my case), the love of parents (two, of course), and the love of a church. For me, this church is the one.

The church. This is God's church, and it is mine. Make that "ours." It had changed over the years, in good ways and bad in my opinion, but that's just my opinion. I've got to remember who is in control. That same concept probably applies to you.

I urge you to remember the sad things. Don't push them out of your mind. Sometimes that's how we learn. But I also ask you to consider the good things. Keep it all in balance. Don't ever forget that love, and a willing acceptance of God's will in our lives and in the life of the church, are two ideas which, to me, are very important. I intend to continue to be a member of this church—a participating member. I don't like the bad times, but I wouldn't miss the good times for anything. And remember, I speak from first-hand experience.

My prayer for you and for me is short, to the point, and no doubt familiar:

Our Father, who art in heaven, hallowed be thy name. Thy kingdom come, thy will be done, on earth.

Amen.

God's Greatest Hits, Volume One

— • —

Ashley, Elizabeth, and Tallu sang a song. The occasion was our church's annual tribute to its graduating high-school seniors. The song they sang was called "Forever Friends."

Ashley, Elizabeth, and Tallu had been close for years. I had seen them together at church quite often, and I'd been told that their relationship went far beyond that. But the time for separation had come, and they chose to mark that milestone with music.

"Forever Friends."

The melody was hauntingly beautiful. The lyrics paid appropriate tribute both to the love these young women felt for one another and to God's eternal love for all three of them.

That song, that honest, intimate declaration of friendship, was a worship service in itself. It filled my spirit to overflowing with joy. Had it been the only thing to happen at church that Sunday, I still would have gone home uplifted and satisfied.

Music can do that to the human soul. Music has the power to fill us, enrich us, empower us, and make us feel better.

Well, not *all* music. Not when I'm the one trying to play it.

How can someone who loves music as much as I do be so totally bereft of musical talent? If I were ever to rub a magic lamp and cause a real live genie to appear, I *definitely* would use one of my three wishes to correct that situation.

For openers, I would ask the genie to teach me how to play the five-string banjo. Let me tell you, that would put his power to the test!

I've always wanted to be able to play an instrument, preferably the banjo, but failing that, the guitar or the piano. But I've never been willing to pay the price. I want to *play* the thing, not *work* at *learning* it.

I took piano lessons when I was six years old. I *quit* taking piano lessons when I was six years old, too. Well, I didn't actually *quit.* The piano belonged to an aunt, and before I could hit my stride on the keyboard, she took it back. She wanted *her* son to take lessons. By the time her son was eighteen, he was writing his own symphonies and operas. He still does that.

Anyway, my "window of opportunity" closed with a thud, and my musical career was put on hold.

I didn't lose my desire, however, and as I stumbled into my teenage years, I found myself intensely envious of any fellow who could sit down at a piano and be the life of the party, basking in the adulation of those who would inevitably gather around and sing along.

Of course I envied the *popularity* that came with the skill more than the skill itself.

After we lost our piano, I didn't sit down at the keyboard again until after Barbara and I were married.

Barbara knew about my lifelong dream, since I had shared it freely, and being a supportive wife, she encouraged me to go for it. She didn't yet know about my talent vacuum. You don't admit something like that until a marriage has been well established.

I signed up for a series of piano lessons with a by-the-book teacher who had the personality of a metronome and was shaped like one as well. For several weeks, I toiled away under her withering stare, struggling up and down the scales in despair. Then, mercifully, I quit the piano a second time.

I was down, but not out.

A ray of hope appeared on my horizon a few years later in the form of a megatalented friend and accomplished pianist who offered her assistance. Displaying patience worthy of sainthood, she led me step-by-step through the notes and chords of two simple Christmas carols. When the holiday arrived, I amazed my family by haltingly hammering out *both* carols while they gathered around and struggled to sing along.

It was a wonderful family moment.

I stopped taking lessons after Christmas and never played the piano again. I no longer *need* to play. Been there, done that.

I didn't give up on music, though. I switched to the guitar and enrolled in adult education lessons at a local high school. The guitar teacher, like my first two piano teachers, had a misguided commitment to teaching the basics. Even worse, he was a classical guitarist, and that's what he wanted *us* to be.

As you may imagine, that experience didn't go well at all. I threw in the towel after a few weeks, without learning a thing.

If you're keeping score, that was my fourth departure from the world of musical instruments.

My dream still wouldn't die, but I gave up the idea of ever learning how to play anything in the presence of other human beings. It was too traumatic. The pressure and the potential for humiliation were too great. There just *had* to be a better way, a less painful way.

While strolling through a music store one day, I found a book which *absolutely guaranteed* I would be playing a song on the guitar by the end of the very first day. Instant gratification was within my reach. I grabbed it.

In a manner of speaking, it worked. The melodious strains of "You Are My Sunshine" filled our house by nightfall. The next day I mastered the suspiciously familiar chords to "On Top of Ole Smoky." After that came "Do Lord" and "I'll Fly Away," once again using the same basic pattern.

I got bored and quit the guitar.

The banjo was next. I didn't try that challenging instrument until I was in my forties and the knuckles of my fingers had begun to stiffen, but that didn't matter. At least I didn't have to choose between an intimidating teacher and a boring, repetitious book. I had discovered a mail order banjo course that came with a book *and* a teacher—on tape, of course.

I ripped open the package the moment it arrived. Soon a mellow voice was pouring from my tape recorder, comforting and encouraging me at the same time. The songs my disembodied teacher played during his demonstration were the kind of bluegrass classics I had always wanted to play. Filled with excitement, I attacked the banjo with gusto.

I should've attacked it with an ax.

In no time I could play *badly*, but I was never able to play *softly*. Let's face it. The banjo is a loud instrument. In fact, the noise got so bad that Barbara made me practice in the backyard, as far away from the house as I could get without being sued by the neighbors.

Being banished took the remaining wind out of my sails. I stored the banjo in the attic, right alongside the guitar.

Okay, so I'm not a player. Nevertheless, I'm an avid listener. I enjoy all kinds of music, but even as a *listener* I have found myself in trouble.

When Barbara and I were married, she wanted to go to New Orleans for our honeymoon. I was a second-year law student, struggling to make ends meet, and I didn't see any way I could handle that kind of expense. Reluctantly, I told her so. We chose a different destination.

I didn't realize at the time that a honeymoon in New Orleans had been her lifelong dream.

Barbara was a remarkably good sport about it, and I promised myself I would make it up to her someday. Ten years later, I seized the moment. I surprised her with two airline tickets to the city of wrought iron and romance.

Our trip was wonderful.

On the evening of our tenth anniversary, our last evening there, we had dinner at a lovely restaurant nestled in an open courtyard. We sat beneath a canopy of trees, with the starry sky hovering above. A gentle breeze, laced with the fragrance of fresh flowers, caressed us ever so softly. Off to one side, a skilled pianist discretely filled the courtyard with romantic melodies.

The music was just the right touch.

We waited patiently for our dinner to arrive. Time didn't matter. There was no place else on earth we would rather be than in that setting, holding hands, watching the glow of the candles dance in each other's eyes. We savored every second.

Barbara smiled and nodded toward the piano player.

"Ask him to play our song," she said softly.

I smiled back, rose obediently, and headed for the piano. As soon as my back was turned, my smile disappeared. I was in a state of total panic.

Our *song*? We have a *song*?

I sidled up to the piano and leaned against it like Humphrey Bogart in *Casablanca*. The pianist didn't stop playing, but he looked up at me inquisitively, wondering what I wanted.

I glanced back in the general direction of my Ingrid

Bergman. She was smiling sweetly, thanking me with her eyes for responding to her request.

Not wanting to look like a total fool, I slipped a dollar into the pianist's snifter. He smiled. I left.

Everyone was happy. Everyone but me.

As I returned to our table, my mind was racing.

"Did he know our song?" Barbara asked hopefully.

I thought about taking the easy way out and telling her he didn't, but my conscience wouldn't let me. Instead, I faced the music, in a manner of speaking.

"I didn't ask him," I admitted glumly.

Barbara was baffled. "Why not?"

I cleared my throat, tugged at my collar, and grinned sheepishly. "Well . . . I didn't know what to ask him to play."

Barbara laughed.

My confidence returned. "I didn't even know we *had* a song!"

Her smile broadened. "Do you remember the movie we saw on our first date?"

Our marriage teetered on the edge of a precipice as I searched my memory for the right answer. Fortunately, it came. I didn't remember the *title*, but I remembered the stars.

"Deborah Kerr and Cary Grant," I ventured.

"*An Affair to Remember*," she confirmed. "That's also the name of our song."

"Of course!" I wasn't about to ask her to hum a few bars. I hurried back to the piano.

It cost me another dollar, but it was worth it. The piano player outdid himself. He played "our song" as it had never been played before, and I heard it with a new awareness.

Our marriage backed away from the precipice and continued on its course.

There was another time when my failure to remember

a song caused a problem, and there are some interesting parallels between the two events. Both began with a request to have a specific song played on a keyboard, and both times, Barbara was the only other person who knew about my dilemma.

It was late May of 1970. A dear friend was dying of cancer. He had demonstrated courage in coming to grips with his death, but some of the rest of us were not so strong.

A few days before he died, he and I were alone together in his hospital room. He told me he wanted to talk about his funeral. I found it difficult to deal with that subject, but at a time like that, you do what you have to do.

"I want y'all to sing the one about the river," he whispered during the course of that conversation. His voice was almost gone, and I could barely hear him.

My first thought was how difficult it would be to sing at a time like that.

"The one about the river?"

"Yeah, the peaceful river." He looked at me pleadingly and struggled to continue. "You know the one—they sing it at funerals." He smiled as if he had let me in on a secret, but then he grimaced in pain.

He didn't say anything else, and I didn't ask any more questions.

As soon as possible, I located a hymnal and began flipping through its pages, looking in vain for a song that fit his extremely skimpy description. I sweated bullets until the day of the funeral, and literally kept on searching up until the moment the service was about to start.

That's when I stumbled across "Jesus Keep Me Near the Cross."

> In the cross, in the cross, be my glory ever,
> till my raptured soul shall find
> rest beyond the river.

That *had* to be it! I showed it to Barbara. She agreed. I alerted the organist. When the time came, we sang as best we could.

I was enormously relieved. My promise to my friend had been kept.

Sixteen years later, the truth was revealed.

I was attending another funeral. Some time during that service, the preacher held up a hymnal and announced that the family had selected some songs. I turned to the page he had indicated, and joined in.

> When peace, like a river, attendeth my way,
> when sorrows like sea billows roll;
> whatever my lot, thou hast taught me to say,
> It is well, it is well, with my soul!

"This one's for you, my friend," I whispered aloud, suddenly realizing that *this* was the song he had wanted. Then I looked around. Fortunately, no one had heard me, and no one had noticed the smile that had found its way to my face in the midst of all that sadness.

Those two incidents had much in common.

Barbara wanted "our song" played on that special evening because that same song had created a feeling of excitement and romance in her heart many years earlier. She wanted to experience those feelings once again. The music would enable her to do it.

My dying friend wanted the song about the "peaceful river." No doubt it was because at some time in his life he had been deeply touched and reassured by its message. He wanted the rest of us to be consoled through our singing.

Music can awaken a full range of human feelings and emotions. It can bring us peace or lead us toward turmoil. It can resurrect a memory or send us into the future. It can lull us to sleep or set our hearts on fire.

This has been true throughout all human existence.

The sixteenth chapter of the First Book of Samuel relates an illustrative incident.

Samuel was the last of the judges. Toward the end of his years of service, the people of Israel began to demand that a king be appointed to rule over them instead of continuing on with the existing unsatisfactory system.

God told Samuel to heed the cry of the people. Samuel did so. He anointed Saul, whom the Lord had sent.

Saul pleased God at first, but not for long. Eventually, God rejected Saul and told Samuel to select another king.

Enter God's choice, David, the youngest son of Jesse.

Samuel responded to God's command and anointed David. When he did so, the Spirit of the Lord came upon the new king, and at the same time, the Spirit left Saul. In its place, a distressing spirit, also from the Lord, began to invade Saul's being.

One of Saul's servants had a solution. He knew, just as we know today, that music could soothe the troubled spirit. He suggested that Saul call David, who was a skilled harpist. David was willing to help.

At the end of the sixteenth chapter of the First Book of Samuel, we learn the result of David's effort:

> And so it was, whenever the spirit from God was upon Saul, that David would take a harp and play it with his hand. Then Saul would become refreshed and well, and the distressing spirit would depart from him.
>
> (16:23 NKJ)

Music has an undeniable power. The music of our faith has the greatest power of all.

When Barbara and I held hands and knelt at the altar, our first act as man and wife, the sound of "The Lord's Prayer" filled our hearts.

"O Divine Redeemer" brings forth the sadness that enveloped me when Barbara's father died, and reminds me of the affection for him that still lingers in my heart. He loved that song so much! I hope the angels sing it for him every day.

"The Church in the Wildwood" is forever linked to my own father. He had a lovely voice, and when I was very young, he sang that song to me. I'm filled with warmth at the thought of it. I treasure that memory.

Whenever I hear the "Hallelujah Chorus," my heart almost explodes with wonder and joy.

When my faith is weak and my need is great, I listen to the hymns and spirituals of Tennessee Ernie Ford. I first heard him sing when I was sixteen years old and filled with the incomparable joy of new faith. Listening to those songs always helps me recapture that excitement.

"What a Friend We Have in Jesus" reminds me of my Savior's boundless love.

"Just as I Am, Without One Plea" brings the peaceful presence of the redeeming grace my Savior extends to sinners like myself.

"Sweet Hour of Prayer" blesses me with a special kind of reassuring peace.

"Onward Christian Soldiers" energizes me with the confident awareness of God's power.

"It Is Well with My Soul," the song about the peaceful river, brings the comforting, calming assurance that in the end, all *will* be well for those of us who truly believe.

My list could go on and on.

No, I can't *play*, but I can *listen*. Musical talent is God's gift to the individual, and he has chosen to give it to someone else. But music's *power*, music's *beauty*, well, that's God's gift to all of us.

I thank Elizabeth, Ashley, and Tallu for singing from their hearts, and for reminding me of that simple truth.

What's Red and White and Known All Over?

— • —

No, THE ANSWER TO THAT RIDDLE IS *NOT* THE University of Alabama football team, although that wouldn't be a bad guess at all.

Paul (Bear) Bryant became a legend as the football coach at Alabama. In the years that followed his death, stories about this extraordinary man circulated widely. Some were true, some were not, but all of them added to his remarkable mystique.

One such story, one likely to be true, was told by a former player. He was a freshman, and he was dressing for his very first game at Tuscaloosa's Bryant-Denney Stadium. On arriving at the locker room, he and the other Bama players found most of their equipment in their lockers, where it was supposed to be, ready to use.

Everything but their game jerseys.

The players said nothing. They simply donned their practice jerseys, which *were* in their lockers, and ran out on the field for their warm-ups. Then they returned to the locker room for a pregame pep talk from their larger-than-life coach.

Bear Bryant remained silent. He strolled around the quiet locker room and made eye contact with each player, one at a time. Then, at the last possible moment, when it was almost time for the players to return to the field, he opened a box and handed each player a bright crimson jersey.

Words weren't necessary. When those players ran out on

the field, they were sky high, filled with pride. They were part of a winning tradition, and their easily recognized jerseys announced it to the world.

Few of us will ever experience a moment as intense as that, but we can identify with those players in some small way. It's always nice to be part of a winning tradition and carry a winner's colors.

But the answer to this riddle *isn't* the Crimson Tide. It's the emblem of the Red Cross, a flag displayed all over the world, day in and day out, wherever human beings are in need. The Red Cross is *always* there, without fail.

This story is about one small part of that worthy organization's work—the giving and receiving of blood. And in a sense it isn't even a story. It's a thank-you note.

The Judeo-Christian history of human existence on earth begins, of course, with the very first line of The First Book of Moses Called Genesis.

> In the beginning God created the heavens and the earth.
> The earth was without form, and void; and darkness was on the face of the deep. And the Spirit of God was hovering over the face of the waters.
> Then God said, "Let there be light"; and there was light.
> And God saw the light, that it was good; and God divided the light from the darkness.
> God called the light Day, and the darkness He called Night. So the evening and the morning were the first day.
> (1:1-5 NKJ)

On the second day, God separated the firmament from the waters, calling the firmament Heaven. On the third day, he gathered the water to its place and let the dry land appear, and called it Earth. After that, he brought forth vegetation. On the fourth day, he created the two great lights and separated day and night, letting the sun illuminate the day and the moon and stars the night. On the fifth day, he created the fish of the sea, the birds of the air, and the creatures that crawl or walk upon the land.

The Bible tells us that at the end of each day, after he had completed each of these miracles, "God saw that it was good."

On the sixth day, God created man, giving him dominion over the creatures of the sea, the land, and the air. Following *that* accomplishment, God looked at all that he had done and pronounced it *"very* good." A subtle difference, perhaps, but clearly indicative of God's regard for the greatest of his creations.

God knew what he was talking about. The inescapable truth is that man, humankind, is a "very good" creation. Man is a miracle. No doubt about it.

In the first chapter of Genesis, at verse twenty-seven, we are told that when God created human, "male and female He created them." In the second chapter of that book, beginning at verse eighteen, we learn more of the details:

> And the LORD God said, "It is not good that man should be alone; I will make him a helper comparable to him." . . .
> And the LORD God caused a deep sleep to fall on Adam, and he slept; and He took one of his ribs, and closed up the flesh in its place.
> Then the rib which the LORD God had taken from man He made into a woman, and He brought her to the man.
> And Adam said:
> > "This is now bone of my bones
> > And flesh of my flesh;
> > She shall be called Woman,
> > Because she was taken out of Man."
> > (2:18, 21-23 NKJ)

Note that only "bones" and "flesh" are specifically mentioned by Adam; there's not a word about blood. So where did Eve's blood come from? Was it Adam's blood? Was it created anew? Rhetorical questions, perhaps, but interesting nevertheless.

The story continues in chapter four, verse one:

> Now Adam knew Eve his wife, and she conceived and bore Cain, and said, "I have gotten a man from the LORD."
> Then she bore again, this time his brother Abel. Now Abel was a keeper of sheep, but Cain was a tiller of the ground.
>
> (4:1-2 NKJ)

Eve gave birth to two sons—first Cain, then Abel. If all the rest of the creation story wasn't amazing enough, along comes that miracle of miracles, the birth of a baby.

Consider what happens at the time of conception.

Deep inside the woman, unseen and unfelt, an egg develops, a minuscule collection of tissues *almost* capable of someday becoming a person. Almost, but not quite.

At just the right time, following an ageless instinct, guided only by the natural rhythm of the woman's body, that egg begins a journey. If love's union has been consummated, another miracle may take place, a one-in-a-million miracle called fertilization.

When *that* happens, the egg is fully capable of fulfilling its destiny.

We have no idea what takes place inside the egg at the moment of fertilization. In spite of the efforts of our best scientists and genetic engineers and others who have tried to figure it out for generations, all we really know is that it *happens*, and afterward the egg is different.

How different?

Just different enough.

The now-different egg inside the woman's body doesn't stay where it was when it was fertilized. It keeps on moving through its warm, dark world, still following its instinct, still in tune with the woman's natural rhythm. Finally it comes to rest, attaching itself to the wall of the woman's womb.

The egg's cells begin to divide. Very soon, it is large enough and complex enough to need nourishment.

All of this happened inside Eve's body after that very first conception.

When the fertilized egg comes to rest and needs nourishment to survive, another miracle occurs. It is the union of mother and child, a lifeline which will exist, if all goes well, for forty weeks.

That lifeline remained intact inside of Eve until Cain was ready to be born.

The union of Eve and Cain, mother and child, was the *very first* blood transfusion. Eve's blood began flowing into Cain's microscopic veins, carrying nourishment and protection, guarding and sustaining his life.

The giving of blood by one human being to another for the purpose of sustaining life is nothing short of a divinely created miracle. Every human being begins life with a transfusion. No human being can exist without the gift of another person's blood.

In August of 1956, sixteen people stepped inside a Red Cross blood collection center, rolled up their sleeves, and gave the gift of life. All then left the center knowing they had done the right thing. They had *no idea* what would happen to that blood.

Some time later that month, a young man was carried into the emergency room at a Nashville hospital. By the time the doctors opened him up, he had almost bled to death.

The call went out. The call was answered. Sixteen pints of fresh blood, given by Red Cross volunteers, were ready for just such an emergency.

I was that young man. Almost forty years later, I am still alive.

At Red Cross Blood Services, and at every other volunteer blood donor facility in the world, the bottom line isn't profit, or even breaking even. It isn't statistics, such as the number of pints collected, or even the number of pints available at any given time. All of that matters, but that's not what it's about.

The bottom line is people—people in crisis who need blood to live and healthy people who care and are willing to roll up their sleeves.

Those who receive blood when they need it often never know the identity of their benefactors. Likewise, those who donate blood probably never know the names of those they have helped. But I can tell you this—*both* will be happier and better off for the experience. For the recipient, the benefit is obvious. For the donor, it is every bit as real. He or she has given a priceless treasure to the one who needs it.

The feeling of satisfaction such a gift can bring its giver is indescribable. The gratitude felt by recipients like myself, who are alive and well because of the generosity of donors, is indescribable, too. My veins still carry the blood of sixteen different people, men and women whose names I will never know, whose faces I will never see.

I thank them from the bottom of my heart.